WITCHCRAFT
in

COLONIAL VIRGINIA

WITCHCRAFT
in
COLONIAL VIRGINIA

CARSON O. HUDSON JR.

THE
History
PRESS

Published by The History Press
Charleston, SC
www.historypress.com

Copyright © 2019 by Carson O. Hudson Jr.
All rights reserved

Front cover, top: John Smith's map of Virginia, 1626. *Library of Congress. Bottom*: *Witch Number 1*, by Joseph E. Baker, 1892. *Library of Congress.*
Back cover, top: *The Nightmare*, by John Henry Fuseli, 1781. *Bottom*: The devil marking his servants, from Francesco Maria Guazzo's *Compendium Maleficarum*, 1608.
Title page: The devil appears. From Francesco Maria Guazzo's *Compendium Maleficarum*, 1608.

First published 2019

Manufactured in the United States

ISBN 9781467144247

Library of Congress Control Number: 2019940047

To the memory of Katherine Grady.

Hanged as a witch, off the coast of Virginia, 1654.

CONTENTS

Contents

PREFACE

Although I was and continue to be primarily a military historian, I began a study of witchcraft many years ago, specifically witchcraft cases in colonial Virginia. In those days, before the internet made resources much more convenient, I laboriously tracked down surviving colonial court documents, obscure books and treatises and every primary and secondary source I could locate. I was always looking for anything that would provide greater detail to the meager legal accounts that I found. I spoke with researchers, scholars, educators and legal historians seeking anyone who could provide me with information, opinions and explanations. All my research eventually resulted in a dramatic work, titled *Cry Witch*, for the Colonial Williamsburg Foundation.

I wasn't satisfied, however. Although actual period records were scarce, I had managed to acquire a lot of interesting background and related information. I also found that modern cultural beliefs about historic witchcraft were filled with myth, local legend and Hollywood's ideas of bad history. The result was I wrote a small book about the actual witchcraft beliefs and court cases that occurred in Virginia. Using a quote from England's King James I, I titled my work *These Detestable Slaves of the Devill*. This, in turn, led me to begin lecturing on the subject, ensuring me speaking engagements every Halloween.

Over the last twenty years, I've met with many people who have attended one of my lectures. Talking with them after a lecture or at a book signing, I've found that for many, Hollywood still seems to be teaching history—but I've also been able to find new contacts with additional historical sources and information.

Arcadia Publishing and The History Press have now given me the opportunity to revise, update and expand my original work. For that I am truly grateful. This new volume represents those efforts, and I hope it will be appreciated by those who wish to distinguish between reality and sensational myths and legends. And of course, I'll still have work at Halloween!

—Carson Hudson
Williamsburg, Virginia
February 2019

ACKNOWLEDGEMENTS

In researching and writing about witchcraft in colonial Virginia, one feels much like the freeholders that comprised the juries of the county courts of the period. First, each instance of witchcraft must be discovered and investigated. Then, research needs to be conducted into the facts of each case. Finally, one must obtain opinions and make decisions regarding what may have actually happened in each case and what is legend or local Virginia folklore of the last three-hundred-plus years.

It would have been impossible to complete my investigations without the help of a number of friends and associates at the Colonial Williamsburg Foundation. They offered assistance, guidance and advice.

Especially valued were the opinions and suggestions of Jeremy Fried and Tom Hay, both fine historians of colonial Virginia law. Abigail Schumann shared her knowledge of seventeenth-century Virginia. Lou Powers and Kevin Kelly of Colonial Williamsburg's research department readily answered my often-strange questions. Gail Greve, Del Moore and Juleigh Clark, along with the rest of the staff of the Rockefeller Library, were of great assistance in locating obscure books and documents. A special thanks to Marianne Martin, who diligently searched for images I might use, and to Bob Ruegsegger, who graciously permitted me to use his photographs.

The helpful staff of the Virginia State Library guided me through an untold number of county records.

A fine historian and old friend, Anna Holloway, reviewed my notes and gave me valuable feedback, as did Anne Marie Millar, who provided constructive criticism.

I would like to thank Arcadia Publishing and especially Kate Jenkins, acquisitions editor of The History Press, who believed in my work. Her guidance through the world of publishing during the creation of this expanded edition of my original work was invaluable.

Finally, I must mention my long-suffering wife, Melissa. Being born in Kansas and a *Wizard of Oz* groupie, she easily tolerates a husband who spends way too much time reading and lecturing about witchcraft.

INTRODUCTION

On April 26, 1607, three small ships, the *Susan Constant*, the *Godspeed* and the *Discovery*, arrived off the coast of Virginia. They brought with them 104 men and boys who would construct a wooden palisade at a spot they called Jamestown, named for their king, James I. Thus, the first permanent English settlement in North America was established. The settlers who arrived on that spring day brought with them their thoughts of home and their cultural beliefs and values. Among their beliefs was the conviction that witches were alive and thriving in the world.

The seventeenth century was an age when witches and demons, alchemists and sorcerers, sea monsters and fanciful creatures were accepted by Englishmen, regardless of their social or intellectual station in life. A brief investigation of the literature and plays of their acquaintance confirms these beliefs. It is illustrated in such well-known pieces as Christopher Marlowe's *Doctor Faustus* (1604) and William Shakespeare's *Midsummer Night's Dream* (1595), *Macbeth* (1605) and *The Tempest* (1611). Similar plays characterizing contemporary beliefs were Thomas Middleton's *The Witch* (1609) and *The Witch of Edmonton* (1621) by Thomas Dekker, John Ford and William Rowley.

Virginia, with its dark forests and strange native inhabitants, must have seemed quite frightening indeed. King James I himself had written that the devil's handiwork was "thought to be most common in such wilde partes of the world." It was there that "the Devill findes greatest ignorance and barbaritie." For at least the next hundred years, Virginians would be on the lookout for the Satan and his followers.

Macbeth's Three Witches, by Henry Fuseli, 1783.

Over the years, much has been written about colonial witchcraft, primarily about the infamous Salem, Massachusetts witch trials. When one thinks of a witch trial in colonial America, the image of a narrow-minded Puritan judge self-righteously presiding over a predisposed court, sentencing dozens of innocent women to death, comes to mind. Actually, although there was a fear of witchcraft in every British colony of the seventeenth and early eighteenth centuries, except for the aberration of the Salem trials, no widespread witch hunts occurred in England's North American colonies.

That does not mean that there were no witchcraft proceedings in Virginia. Throughout the period, there were a number of examinations into accusations of witchcraft and sorcery. However, the justices who conducted these examinations tended to act with a more cautious approach in the prosecution of those who were suspected of being in league with the devil.

Unfortunately, because of wars and neglect, many of Virginia's colonial documents and records have been lost. What survives is an incomplete record at best. Over time, stories of alleged witchcraft have been embellished with folklore and legend to produce tales that are amusing for the readers of ghost stories and mysteries but have little or no historical truth.

This volume is intended to be a survey of the surviving records and known facts about the time when early Virginians imagined Satan to be walking among them.

I

THE BELIEFS

Being a Brief Description of Some of the Witchcraft Beliefs of the Early Inhabitants of Colonial Virginia

By the pricking of my thumbs, Something wicked this way comes.
—William Shakespeare, Macbeth *Act IV, Scene I*

BELIEFS ABOUT WITCHES

What is a witch?

It is popularly accepted today that a witch is defined as someone who employs witchcraft in the form of magic, spells or potions for specific aims, good or bad. Notwithstanding this, we tend to associate witches with the familiar images of black pointed hats, cats and old hags flying on brooms. Except for Halloween and the occasional movie or television program, most people don't often think about witches. It is hard to imagine a time when the idea of witches as servants of the devil was a seriously accepted belief. It was mentioned in the Bible, and educated men wrote volumes of literature concerning the activities and traits of supposed witches.

The idea of witchcraft goes back to ancient times, but the word *witch* does not always appear in ancient languages. There were magicians, soothsayers, diviners, fortune-tellers, folk healers and such, but more times than not, the practitioners of those arts were not considered evil. They were productive and valued members of their local communities. In early modern England, these individuals were considered "cunning folk" and a necessary part of daily life. A herbalist, midwife or healer was thought

Wicked Witch of the West from *The Wizard of Oz*, 1939. *Wikimedia Commons.*

of only as a neighbor who possessed special skills valued by a community and consulted with as one today would take their problems to a local physician, pharmacist, nurse practitioner or veterinarian. Folk magic was ever present.

Beginning around the fourteenth century, the Catholic Church began to classify folk magic and "cunning folk" as witchcraft. Those who didn't fit in with proper religious doctrine began to be associated with heresy, evil and the devil.

Historically speaking, this is where evil or Satanic witchcraft as it is thought of today begins. The definition of a witch became someone who used magic exclusively to cause harm.

This in turn prompted the stimuli for European outbreaks of "witch hunts" or "witch manias." While tragic, popular imagination and legend have exaggerated the extent and ferocity of the outbreaks and executions that occurred during these persecutions. Some sources claim that victims were in the millions; however, scholars today generally contend that the actual number of victims was lower and the number varied by location. Influenced by war, drought, famine and religion, the worst panics and executions took place in select areas, notably in southern Germany, while there were virtually no accusations of witchcraft in Ireland. In general, although there was a wide-ranging and complete folklore about witches and demons, one British historian has observed that three-quarters of Europe did not witness a single witch trial.

So, what did early Virginians believe about witches?

There were certain generally accepted beliefs and superstitions related to the lives and activities of witches. Although there were always some persons who did not adhere to various viewpoints or tales, it is

An English woodcut of the devil appearing to a woman. *Public domain.*

An ancient witch as an oracle. *The Magic Circle* by John William Waterhouse, 1886.

Witches dancing with the devil. From Francesco Maria Guazzo's *Compendium Maleficarum*, 1608.

Satan's servants signing the devil's book. From Francesco Maria Guazzo's *Compendium Maleficarum*, 1608.

safe to say that these beliefs went back to the British Isles and were familiar among the early settlers in Virginia, who brought these notions with them as surely as they brought the clothes on their backs.

According to common opinion at the time, no one was born a witch. They were ordinary human beings who had forsaken baptism and sworn allegiance to Satan. They had made a pact with the devil, signed their name in his black book and received his mark on their bodies. In return, they acquired powers to cause mischief and harm. They used curses and spells to ruin crops, spoil milk, cause storms and sicken livestock. They delighted in plaguing, crippling or even killing innocent men, women and children.

DEVIL'S MARKS

A common popular belief was that when a witch made a pact with the devil, he would mark that person with a hot iron or his tongue, thereby leaving "the devil's mark." But even the most learned scholars of the period were unable to agree on exactly what a devil's mark consisted of. Opinions varied, but it was commonly thought that the marks were in secret places such as armpits or "private partes." They were considered to be impervious to pain and, sometimes, unable to bleed. An examination for witchcraft would often include a search for such marks, and every mole, birthmark, blemish and scar would come under close scrutiny.

Satan, purportedly, would also give each witch an extra teat or nipple, so that a familiar, or demon servant, could nourish themselves on a witch's blood. This was known as the "witch's mark" or "witch's teat." Also called "biggs" or "titts," the term *witch's mark* was often used interchangeably with *devil's mark*. Because devil's or witch's marks were considered to have no feeling, an examiner could detect a witch by sticking a suspicious mark with a pin or "pricker." A "pricking test" would consist of a suspected individual being blindfolded while a pin or needle was stuck in suspected

The devil marking his servants From Francesco Maria Guazzo's *Compendium Maleficarum*, 1608.

marks. If no pain or effect was observed, then the mark was considered to be preternatural.

In 1705, John Bell, a Scottish minister, wrote a discourse in which he described his experience with a witch's mark:

> *This mark is sometimes like a little Teate; sometimes like a blewish spot: and I myself have seen it in the body of a confessing Witch like a little powder mark of a blea colour, somewhat hard, and withal insensible, so as it did not bleed when I pricked it.*

The use of torture to discover a witch or gain a confession was technically illegal in England and, accordingly, in Virginia. Pricking, however, was considered not to be torture, but a test.

Virginia courts were known to have ordered examinations for devil's or witch's marks on several occasions. Usually, the magistrates would take

The Obscene Kiss. The devil's servants paying homage. From Francesco Maria Guazzo's *Compendium Maleficarum*, 1608.

care to ensure that any jury formed to search for such marks would have some knowledge of the body, so that normal and natural body marks would not be mistaken for a pact with the devil. In the 1706 case of Grace Sherwood, for example, the Princess Anne County Court prescribed that the jury impaneled to search her person was to be composed of "ancient and knowing women." The juries were to be of the same sex as the person accused and, in the case of a woman, to have at least one midwife present rather than a doctor.

A jury of women impaneled to examine the body of a suspected witch was a jury of inquiry, not a trial jury. They were a fact-finding body, comparable to a coroner's jury, but their findings did not possess the dignity of a verdict.

FAMILIARS

A familiar was a demon servant of a supposed witch that would assist in carrying out spells, bewitchments and mischief.

Once again, there was disagreement during the colonial period regarding how a witch actually obtained a familiar. Some believed that familiars were demons given to new witches by the devil when they sold their souls. Others held that familiars were the product of a magical spell and that they received their power from the witch and not the devil.

Also known as a familiar spirit or imp, these familiars would usually assume the shape of a small animal, such as cats, dogs, toads, owls or

A witch and her familiars. From *A Rehearsall both Straung and True, of Hainous and Horrible Actes Committed by Elizabeth Stile*, 1579.

A cat as a familiar. From *A Rehearsall both Straung and True, of Hainous and Horrible Actes Committed by Elizabeth Stile*, 1579.

mice. Still another notion held that these familiars were otherwise normal animals that had been bewitched. Since any animal or even insect could be a familiar, it was consequently quite easy for an examining authority to find some household pet or vermin that could be considered in league with an accused witch.

It was also believed that the familiars craved blood as payment for their services. Witches would reward them with their own blood by suckling a familiar with their witch's teat or mark. A particular proof to detect a witch's teat was the test "by stool." In this examination, an accused witch would be bound to a chair or stool in an empty room and constantly observed for a set period of twenty-four hours or more. It was felt that a witch's familiar would be forced to return for a daily feeding and therefore expose the witch.

Most treatises on the subject would list both a witch's mark and a familiar as a proof of witchcraft.

HAG RIDING OR FLYING

While not unanimously accepted, many alleged that witches possessed the ability to fly from place to place. This survives to the present day with the image of a witch riding on a broom. Interestingly enough, reports of witches flying on broomsticks are almost totally absent from English witch trials. When there is a mention of flying, a shovel, hayfork or basket is used more often than a broom; in Scotland, it appears supposed witches employed bean and straw stalks. In Germany, it was thought witches used forked sticks or demons.

It was also assumed that a witch might bewitch and ride a horse or other farm animal for flight. If a "mare" was unavailable, a witch, or "hag," could climb on the back of a human who was then made to gallop about at the witch's command. Since such activities always took place at night, they became known as "night-mares."

Victims of such a nightmarish excursion often described feelings of falling, great weights on the body or even suffocation. Such a victim was said to have been "ridden" or "hag ridden."

Today, such symptoms are identified as a modern sleep disorder known as "sleep paralysis." This medical condition occurs when someone is attempting to fall asleep or just waking up. The victim is aware of their surroundings but unable to move or speak. They may experience a feeling of suffocation or chest pressure and delusionary visions such as falling or flying. Some sufferers claim to hear noises or voices. Often the results of these sensory overloads are fear and panic attacks. Notably, these

Witches on broomsticks. From *The History of Witches and Wizards*, 1720.

Etching of two witches on a broom by Francisco Goya, 1797–98.

Left: A witch flying on a goat. From Francesco Maria Guazzo's *Compendium Maleficarum*, 1608.

Below: *The Nightmare*, by John Henry Fuseli, 1781.

symptoms seem to match colonial courtroom descriptions of supposed witchcraft victims.

There were some who assumed that a witch needed a special "flying ointment" in order to fly. This ointment was rumored to be given to witches when they signed their pact with the devil.

A curious custom that does not seem to have made it to Virginia was the belief that church bells would counteract the power of a witch to fly.

In England and continental Europe, it was sometimes the practice to ring church bells to prevent witches from flying overhead.

Early Virginians seemed to have been afflicted by hag riding, as it is mentioned in several witchcraft accusations throughout the colonial period.

SEA STORMS

A witch causing a storm. From Olaus Magnus's *Historia de gentibus Septentrionalibus*, 1555.

A commonly held belief of colonial Virginians was that a witch had the power to create a storm at sea and control the wind and rain. A witch that controlled the winds and rain, affected the ability to catch fish or influenced the tides was sometimes known as a sea hag.

At least three women were executed for being witches aboard ships that were involved in violent storms in or near Virginia waters. It is interesting to note, however, that it was the captain and crew of the vessels who executed, or lynched, those unfortunate women, rather than the proper legal authorities.

Nevertheless, even the learned among Virginia's gentry believed in the power of witches to cause or prevent a sea storm. It was thought that one should always keep in the good graces of anyone who might influence a sea voyage. A 1735 letter from William Byrd II to a London merchant stated, "I am glad to hear your ship the *Williamsburg* got home well, and that Crane [the captain] agreed with a witch at Hampton for a fair wind all the way."

In England and continental Europe, it was also thought that groups of witches could control the weather in order to ruin agricultural crops and harm local economies. This was known in those areas as "weather witching." There is no mention of any similar suspected activity in Virginia records.

PUPPETS

The practice of creating a human image is older than the belief in Satanic witchcraft and has been documented in every part of the world and in all ages of history. Ordinary folk might use a figurine or image to provoke either love or harm on an intended recipient. To colonial Virginians, puppets (or poppets) were dolls, believed to have been made in the image of a person who was the object of a spell or curse. They could be made out of wood, wax or dough and included small bits of clothing, locks of hair or nail clippings of the victim.

Supposedly, since the puppet was bound to a particular person through magic by the use of a personal item, they would contain the essence of that person. Actions against the puppet or figure, such as piercing with pins or nails, burning with a candle or even hanging, would in some way affect the intended victim. In 1560, Queen Elizabeth I was apparently the intended victim when a female wax image with a pin thrust through it was discovered in a public square in London.

In his book *Daemonologie*, written in 1597, King James VI of Scotland (later King James I of England) detailed how witches would cause harm to their victims:

> *To some others at these times he* [the devil] *teacheth how to make pictures of wax or clay. That by the roasting thereof, the persons that they beare the name of, may be continually melted or dried away by continual sickness.*

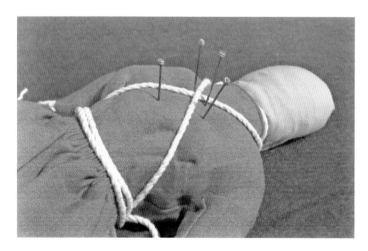

A reconstructed Elizabethan witch's "poppet" pierced with brass pins. *Author's collection.*

26

Early Virginians were familiar with, and believed in, a witch's use of puppets. In both the 1675 case of Joan Jenkins and the 1706 case of Grace Sherwood, county courts ordered that their houses be searched for "Images." Dalton's *Country Justice*, which was used as a legal reference by Virginia courts, reiterated King James's warnings:

> *They have often Pictures of Clay or Wax (like a Man, etc., made of such as they would bewitch) found in their House, or which they roast, or bury in the Earth, that as the Picture consumes, so may the parties bewitched consume.*

TRANSFORMATION OR METAMORPHOSIS

The belief that witches could transform themselves into nonhuman forms or animals is closely related to the belief in lycanthropy or werewolves, which was more of a continental European belief. Colonial Virginians seemed to think that witchcraft transformations were more discreet.

In order to spread mischief or cause torment to a victim, a witch was believed to be able to transform into such creatures as a cat or toad. More common was the belief that a witch might transform him or herself to move about undetected or to escape pursuit. This might take the form of a dog or cat, goat, deer or rabbit.

In at least one Virginia case in Princess Anne County in 1698, mention of a supposed transformation was made. A woman of the county, Elizabeth Barnes, declared that Grace Sherwood had visited her house and left by disappearing out the keyhole "like a black Catt."

SWIMMING OR DUCKING

According to some authorities of the colonial period, witches would be repelled by water because they had thrown off the waters of baptism. Therefore, a suspected witch could be discovered if she was placed into a body of water. This was known as "swimming" or "ducking" a witch. King James, an advocate of the test, explained what would happen:

It is a certain rule Witches deny their Baptism when they make Covenant with the Devill, water being the sole element thereof, and when they are heaved into the water it refuseth to receive them but suffers them to float.

Thus, if an accused witch had made a pact with Satan, she would float on the water; if innocent, she would sink. Interestingly enough, although used to discern if a witch had forsaken baptism, the test dated back to the Babylonian Code of Hammurabi (before the practice of baptism):

If anyone brings an accusation against a man, and the accused goes to the river and leaps into the river, if he sinks in the river his accuser shall take possession of his house. But if the river proves that the accused is not guilty, and he escapes unhurt, then he who had brought the accusation shall be put to death, while he who leaped into the river shall take possession of the house that had belonged to his accuser.

Its use as a specific test for witches began in the German region of Westphalia in the mid-sixteenth century. Although used in England, especially during the civil war period of the 1640s, it was generally opposed by assize judges in England and never had a formal legal status. It was, as noted however, endorsed by King James I.

In the actual test, the accused would be stripped down and bound, hands to feet. Sometimes the victim would be put into a porous bag or tied in a bed sheet. Ropes would be tied around her waist, and she would be thrown into a nearby lake or pond. If the accused sank and proved their innocence, then the ropes would be used to save the accused from drowning by pulling them from the water.

The only known witchcraft case in which the test was used in Virginia was during the examination of Grace Sherwood of Princess Anne County in 1706. Located in the present-day city of Virginia Beach is a street still named "Witchduck Road," near the spot where Grace was "tried by water."

The manner of binding a suspected witch for a ducking test. *Wikimedia Commons.*

WITCHES SABBAT OR WITCHES SABBATH

A common European belief that never really took hold in Virginia was the notion of a witches sabbat or sabbath. As described in Francesco Guazzo's *Compendium Maleficarum* (1626), this was a purported gathering of witches presided over by the devil. In popular imagination, these meetings would occur late at night, usually in a deep forest clearing. There would be a central bonfire around which the witches would dance with Satan. Sometimes the devil would appear in the form of a goat or other animal and sometimes in the form of a black man or man dressed in black.

The Witches Sabbath by Francisco Goya, 1797–98.

Satan accepting a dead child as a sacrifice. From Francesco Maria Guazzo's *Compendium Maleficarum*, 1608.

Other common ideas of the sabbat involved the killing and eating of babies or young children, group sex and worshiping the devil.

It is noteworthy that communities in England only suspected a witches sabbat as having taken place when there were several alleged witches. In colonial Virginia, there were never any mass witch hunts or accusations. Consequently, there is no mention of any supposed witches sabbats in Virginia records.

PROTECTIONS AGAINST WITCHES

Horseshoes

A widespread superstition of the colonial period that has survived into the present day is the belief that horseshoes are good luck amulets and ward off evil.

Horseshoe nailed on a door for good luck. If it was nailed in reverse, it was considered a protection from witchcraft and evil spirits. *Wikimedia Commons.*

The Devil and a Horseshoe, woodcut illustration by George Cruikshank, 1871.

Englishmen of the seventeenth century considered a horseshoe to be a powerful talisman. If nailed over a door or window, they could supposedly prevent a witch from entering a dwelling. If placed in a chimney, they prevented witches from flying in. When nailed to a bedstead, they prevented bewitchments and nightmares. They could even be nailed to the mast of a vessel to keep a ship from harm.

The belief of an iron horseshoe having power over evil dates to a tenth-century legend concerning Saint Dunstan. Before becoming the archbishop of Canterbury, Dunstan apparently was a blacksmith, when one day the devil appeared and asked to have shoes put on his horse. Realizing that his customer was Satan, Dunstan proceeded to nail a horseshoe on the devil's foot, immobilizing him and causing great pain. Eventually, Dunstan agreed to remove the shoe and release the devil if he would promise to never enter any household with a horseshoe nailed over a door or hearth.

In practice, the horseshoe would be positioned with the ends pointed down in order to protect against witchcraft. If the ends were pointed up, the horseshoe became a good luck charm. In 1626, testimony taken in Jamestown during a witchcraft inquiry described how a woman heated a horseshoe in an oven until it was red-hot and then flung it into urine to make a witch "sick at the harte." Another reference of a horseshoe as protection against witches in colonial Virginia appears in a test of a suspected witch in Northumberland County in 1671.

Amulets

Coming from the Latin word *amuletum*, meaning "to drive away or protect," amulets were charms whose purpose was to guard against evil. They could be worn around the neck, placed in a pocket or sewn into clothing. Other placements might be a doorway, hearth, barn or ship's mast. An English and colonial protection against witchcraft was the use of a "hag stone" or stone with a hole through it. If hung on a bedpost at night, it would protect a sleeping person from being ridden.

Small items made of lead or iron were also considered protection against witches. Also common were small pieces of paper with biblical passages or the Lord's Prayer written on them, which could be carried in a small bottle, pocket or locket.

A protective jet pendant amulet from England. *Lincolnshire County Council, Wikimedia Commons*

Protection Spells or Saws

Certain sayings, and rhymes, known as saws, were (and still are) sometimes used as verbal talismans, counter-spell or mantra against evil. They were repeated as a prayer or catechism to protect against witches and demons. In order to be effective, these saws needed to be repeated from memory rather than read, so many of them were in the form of an easily remembered rhyme. Repeating the Lord's Prayer was considered a powerful talisman. The Anglican Book of Common Prayer contains the following litany:

> *From all evil and mischief;*
> *from sin, from the crafts and assaults of the devil;*
> *from thy wrath, and from everlasting damnation,*
> *Good Lord, deliver us.*

A modern corruption of this from a supposedly much older Scottish proverb is:

From Ghoolies and Ghoosties,
long-leggety Beasties, and Things
that go Bump in the Night,
Good Lord, deliver us.

An example of these saws survives today in a popular children's bedtime prayer:

Now I lay me down to sleep, I pray the Lord my soul to keep.
If I should die before I wake, I pray the Lord my soul to take.

Witch Bottles

In seventeenth-century England, many people used witch bottles to counteract the presence of a witch or their spells. Until the early eighteenth century the most common bottle seems to have been a style of glazed German stoneware known as a "Bellarmine" jar or "Bartmann" jug; however, glass bottles and flasks were also used. In the bottle would be placed various combinations of human or animal urine, nails, pins, nail clippings, hair and so forth.

According to common belief, the bottle symbolized the witch's bladder, and the enclosed objects would cause the witch to experience agonizing pain. If such a container was buried under a door, window or hearth, a witch would be unable to enter a household to cause mischief.

Several period treatises gave assorted instructions on the manufacture and use of witch bottles. In a 1701 article on how to prepare a witch bottle, Jason Semmens wrote:

[T]ake about a pint of your owne Urine and make it almost scalding hot then Emtie it into a stone Jugg with a narrow Mouth then put into it so Much white Salt as you can take up with the Thumb and two forefingers of your lift hand and three new nails with their points down wards, their points being first made very sharp then stop the mouth of the Jugg very close with a piece of Tough clay and bind a piece of Leather firm over the stop then put the Jugg into warm Embers and keep him there 9 or 10 days and

A Bellarmine jug of the
type used as a witch bottle.
*Metropolitan Museum of Art,
Wikimedia Commons.*

*nights following so that it go not stone cold all that mean time day nor night
and your private Enemies will never after have any power upon you either
in Body or Goods, So be it.*

Several witch bottles dating from the seventeenth through the late
nineteenth centuries have been recovered at archaeological sites in
England. Similar finds have been unearthed in Virginia, Maryland
and Pennsylvania. In 1979, archaeologists working on a seventeenth-
century house site near Great Neck Point in Virginia Beach discovered
an inverted glass vial, suspected to be a witch bottle, filled with brass pins
in a yellowish liquid.

Another known protection was a "witch box." Popular in sixteenth- and
seventeenth-century England, they were usually wooden boxes with glass
fronts. Inside would be placed herbs, pins, bones and other miscellany

Collection of concealed shoes from East Anglia, England, held by St. Edmundsbury Heritage Service, St Edmundsbury Borough Council. *Wikimedia Commons.s*

over which a magic spell was cast, in the hopes of discouraging witches and evil.

A curious related custom was the use of shoes, concealed in fireplaces and chimneys of a house, assumed to ward off witches and evil. It is possible, however, these shoe concealments were instead meant to be more of a good luck tradition than witchcraft deterrent. Discoveries of "shoe concealment" have been made during the renovation and restoration of various colonial buildings in Virginia.

II

THE LAW

Consisting of the More Notable Legal Statutes and Opinions Regarding Witchcraft as They Affected the Colony of Virginia

The Existence of Witches…has been a Subject of controversy among learned Men.…But nevertheless, 'tis a Capital Offence.
—*George Webb,* The Office and Authority of a Justice of Peace, *1736*

Colonial Virginians had a four-tiered system of courts. First, there were single magistrates, or justices of the peace, who could act summarily, as in small claims cases. Next, there were the local county courts, which consisted of at least four justices of the peace (a quorum) sitting on the bench on established court days. These courts of record heard matters of property, settled simple disputes and held examining courts.

Felony matters were serious enough that the punishment was death by hanging. By the eighteenth century, felonious cases involving slaves could be held at the county level, but during the seventeenth and eighteenth centuries, there was only one court in Virginia that could hear a felony case that involved a white defendant. This was the General Court.

Those accused of a felonious crime, such as witchcraft, were tried by this court, which was presided over by the royal governor and his council. The governor would serve as the chief justice on any felonious witchcraft-related cases that came before the court.

Throughout the colonial period, the governor of Virginia was appointed by either the British Crown or, during the period of the English Commonwealth (1652–60), selected by the Virginia House of Burgesses.

Dramatic reenactment of a witchcraft examination. *Courtesy of Bob Ruegsegger.*

Several of the governors never actually set foot in Virginia, however, and others left the colony for various lengths of time. For most of the period, the General Court was actually presided over by lieutenant governors or senior members of the governor's council. From 1626 until the mid-eighteenth century (the period covered by this volume), the men who governed Virginia were:

Sir George Yeardley (1626–27), governor, died in office
Francis West (1627–29), governor elected by the council
John Potts (1629–30), governor elected by the council

Sir John Harvey (1630–35), governor

John West (1635–37), governor elected by the council

Sir John Harvey (1637–39), governor

Sir Francis Wyatt (1639–42), governor

Sir William Berkeley (1642–52), governor

Richard Kemp (1644–45) president of council, acting governor during absence of Sir William Berkeley

Richard Bennett (1652–55), governor elected by the assembly

Edward Digges (1655–56), governor elected by the assembly

Samuel Matthews (1656–60), governor elected by the assembly

Sir William Berkeley (1660), governor elected by the assembly

Sir William Berkeley (1660–77), governor

Francis Moryson (1661–62), lieutenant governor, acting governor during the absence of Sir William Berkeley

Thomas Culpeper (1677–83), governor

Herbert Jeffreys (1677–78), lieutenant governor

Sir Henry Chicheley (1678–82), deputy governor

Nicholas Spencer (1683–84), president of council, acting governor

Francis Howard, Baron Howard of Effingham (1683–92), governor

Nathaniel Bacon Sr. (1684, 1687, 1689–90), president of council, acting governor during absence of Francis Howard

Francis Nicholson (1690–92), lieutenant governor

Sir Edmund Andros (1692–98), governor

Ralph Wormeley (1698), president of council, acting governor during absence of Sir Edmond Andros

Francis Nicholson (1698–1705), governor

William Byrd (1700, 1703, 1704), president of council, acting governor during absences of Francis Nicholson

Edward Nott (1705–6), governor, died in office

Edmund Jenings (1706–8), president of council, acting governor

Robert Hunter (1707–9), governor, captured by French privateers, never arrived

Edmund Jenings (1708–10), lieutenant governor

George Hamilton, Earl of Orkney (1710–37), governor, never came to Virginia

Alexander Spotswood (1710–22), lieutenant governor

Hugh Drysdale (1722–26), lieutenant governor, died in office

Robert Carter (1726–27), president of council, acting governor

Sir William Gooch (1727–49), lieutenant governor

Reconstructed capitol building in Colonial Williamsburg. It was in this building that the eighteenth-century General Court of Virginia would sit. *Wikimedia Commons.*

Until 1699, the General Court was located at Jamestown, at which time it was moved with the capitol to Williamsburg. Finally, the highest level of the legal system was the king, but cases from Virginia rarely reached that point.

Accusations of witchcraft would normally originate in a county court. If the county justices found no evidence, or if the supposed witchcraft was not considered serious enough, the matter would end there with a simple judgment. On the other hand, if the evidence warranted, or if the charge was of a felonious nature, then the accused would be sent to the capital, to the General Court, under the care of a sheriff. There the king's (or queen's) attorney would represent the Crown, as the accused attempted to disprove the allegations against themselves.

As in all felony cases, the testimony of two witnesses was required for a conviction. This presented a problem in witchcraft cases in that the relationship between the devil and a witch was, by definition, hidden or invisible. A witness would rarely, if ever, observe an accused witch actually performing an act of witchcraft. Instead, evidence would consist of the effects of a witch's power, apparitions, familiars and specters or "spectral evidence."

Legally speaking, Virginia courts were following English law and statutes. In practice, English law and statutes were interpreted as needed and became "Virginia Law."

THE WITCHCRAFT ACTS

It was during the reign of King Henry VIII that the English Parliament passed its first witchcraft statute, the Witchcraft Act of 1542. It defined witchcraft as a felony, punishable by death and the forfeiture of the convicted felon's goods and chattels. Before that time, witchcraft accusations in England had been handled primarily by ecclesiastical courts. In addition, the Act of 1542 denied "benefit of clergy" from any person convicted of witchcraft. (See "Benefit of Clergy," page 51)

The act specifically outlawed the

> *use devise practise or exercise, or cause to be devysed practised or exercised, any Invovacons or cojuracons of Sprites witchecraftes enchauntementes or sorceries to the entent to fynde money or treasure or to waste consume or destroy any persone in his bodie membres, or to pvoke* [provoke] *any persone to unlawfull love, or for any other unlawfull intente or purpose.*

The Act of 1542 was repealed only five years later by Henry's son, Edward VI. Section 3 of An Acte for the Repeale of Certain Statutes, 1547, stated:

> *And be it further ordeyned and enacted by thauctoritie aforesaide that all offences made felonye by anny acte or actes of plament statute or statutes made sithins the xxiij daie of Apryll in the first yere of the reigne of the saide late Kynge Henry theight. Not being felonye before and also all and everye the braunches and articles mentioned or in anny wise declared in anny of the same statute concerning the making of any offence or offences to be felonye not being felonye before, and all paynes and forfaitures concerning the same or anny of them, shalle be hensfurthe be repealed and utterly voide and none effecte.*

During the reign of Queen Elizabeth I, a second act was passed, the Act of 1563. Titled An Act Against Conjurations, Enchantments and Witchcrafts, it was influenced by the witchcraft manias occurring on the continent. The Act of 1563 was more lenient toward those found guilty of witchcraft as opposed to the previous Act of 1542. It continued the prohibition of benefit of clergy, and conviction would result in execution only where harm against persons or property could be proven. The act stated:

Henry VIII, by Hans Holbein the Younger, 1497. *Wikimedia Commons.*

Queen Elizabeth I, about 1575. *Public domain, Wikimedia Commons.*

If any person or persons after the saide first day of June shall use, practise or exercise Witchcraft, enchantment or sorcery, whereby any person shall happen to be killed or destroyed, they shall suffer pains of death as Felon or Felons.

A conviction of anything less, such as fortune-telling or seeking lost treasure, resulted in a misdemeanor, punishable by whipping or imprisonment. Part of the statute concerned the invocation and conjuration of evil spirits for any purpose. The use of "seditious words and rumours" was included, which linked witchcraft with the fashioning of wax figures, the creation of nativities and divining or foretelling the length of royal reigns. This was purposely directed at Catholics.

Coincidentally, the Scottish Parliament enacted a separate Witchcraft Act of 1563, which made the practice of witchcraft and consulting with witches a felony.

The third major witchcraft statute, and the one that was to affect the early Virginia settlers, was the Act of 1604, or the Witchcraft Statute of James I.

STATUTE OF JAMES I

In 1589, the intended bride of King James VI of Scotland, Princess Anne of Denmark, was prevented from crossing over the North Sea by a terrible storm. Personally embarking to retrieve her, the king encountered an even more violent storm that caused the delay of the couple in returning to Scotland. It was rumored that Danish witches caused the king's difficulties.

In the aftermath of several trials and amid the confessions of suspected witches in both Denmark and Scotland, King James became convinced that the devil was out to destroy him. In North Berwick, the devil supposedly met with ten witches and approved an image of James wrapped in linen that was intended to be roasted. According to

King James I of England by Daniel Mytens, 1621. *Wikimedia Commons.*

Anne of Denmark by John De Critz, 1605. *Wikimedia Commons.*

one confession, Satan had declared, "James was the greatest enemy he ever had." The king began a serious study of witchcraft and personally examined some accused witches. A scholarly man, he published a philosophical treatise on the subject titled *Daemonologie* in 1597.

Because of his staunch beliefs, when he came to the throne of England in 1603 as James I, he enacted a new witchcraft statute. Adopted by Parliament in 1604, the Witchcraft Statute of James I was essentially a rewriting of the Statute of 1563; however, it created a wider interpretation of the activities of supposed witches and prescribed harsher punishments for those convicted. It also contained a new element, with sacrilege against a gravesite becoming a felony.

The act divided the crime into two "degrees." Witchcraft of the first degree included causing death or destruction through the conjuration of an evil spirit or the use of charms or sorcery. Punishment for such a conviction was death by hanging. Second degree, or "petit," witchcraft was defined as offering to find buried treasure, locate stolen goods or use potions or charms to provoke "unlawful love." For the first offense of "petit" witchcraft, punishment was a year's imprisonment and being placed in a public pillory every three months, where the convicted would openly confess their offenses. A second conviction would bring a death sentence.

When the first colonists arrived at Jamestown in 1607, they were subject to British statutes, and consequently the Witchcraft Statute of James I was applied to such matters appearing before Virginia courts.

THE COUNTRY JUSTICE

In 1618, Michael Dalton published a summary of English law titled *The Country Justice: Conteyning the Practise of the Justices of the Peace Out of Their Sessions, Gathered for the Better Helpe of Such Justices of Peace as Have Not Beene Much Conversant in the Studie of the Lawes of this Realme.*

Since there was no requirement that one must possess a legal education to become a justice of the peace, Dalton's work was intended as a handbook for those who sat on the bench. The book went through twenty editions between 1618 and 1746. It was well received in Virginia and was used extensively by county court clerks and justices of the peace. *The Country Justice* was found in the law libraries of many Virginians throughout the entire colonial period. It offered advice and legal examples of criminal activities that a justice of the peace might be exposed to, such as murder, rape, horse theft, vagrancy, perjury, property disputes and more.

In his book, Dalton placed the subject of witchcraft under the heading of "Conjuration," which was inserted in "Felonics by Statute." He listed nine types of activities that were punishable under the law:

> *Conjuration, or Invocation of any evill spirit, for any intent, &c. or to be counselling or aiding thereto, is felony, without benefit of Clergy. See Exod.22.18.*
>
> *To consult, covenant with, entertaine, imploy, feede, or reward any evill spirit, is felonie in such offenders, their aydors, and counsellers.*
>
> *To take up any dead body, or any part thereof to be imploied or used in any maner of witchcraft, is felony in such offenders, their aydors, and counsellers.*
>
> *Also to use or practice Witchcraft, Inchantment, Charme, or Sorcery, whereby any person shall be killed, pined, or lamed in any part of their body, or to be counseling or aiding thereto, is felony.*
>
> *Also the second time to practice Witchcraft, &c. thereby to declare where any treasure may be found.*
>
> *Or where any goods lost, or stollen, may be found.*
>
> *Or wherby any cattel or goods shalbe destroied or impaired.*
>
> *Or to the intent to provoke any person to love.*
>
> *Or to the intent to hurt any person in their body, though it be not effected. All these are felony, the second offence; and without benefit of Clergy.*

Dalton went on to provide a guide for gathering evidence of witchcraft by referring to an English assize case of 1612:

> *Now against these witches the Justices of peace may not alwaies expect direct evidence, seeing all their works are the works of darknesse, and no witnesses present with them to accuse them; And therefore their better discovery, I thought good here to insert certain observations out of the book of discovery of the witches that were arraigned at Lancaster, Ann.*

The Country Justice:

CONTAINING

The PRACTICE, DUTY and POWER

OF

The Juſtices of the Peace,

As well in as out of

THEIR SESSIONS.

By MICHAEL DALTON of Lincolns-Inn, Eſq; *And one of the Maſters in* Chancery.

WHEREIN

All the STATUTES in Force and Uſe from *Magna Charta* 9 *Hen.* III. to 15 & 16 *Geo.* II. and alſo All the CASES in LAW, relating to the Juriſdiction and Authority of Juſtices of the Peace, are carefully collected and digeſted under proper Titles.

AND

For the better Help of ſuch JUSTICES of PEACE as have not been much converſant in the Study of the LAWS of this REALM, there is added,

An APPENDIX;

BEING

A Compleat Summary of all the Acts of Parliament, ſhewing the various Penalties of Offences by STATUTE, and the particular Power of **One, Two, Three,** or more Juſtices, in their Proceedings and Determinations, under ſeveral diſtinct Heads, in Alphabetical Order.

With **Four Tables,**

The Firſt, of the Heads of the Chapters. **The Second,** of All the Statutes relating to Juſtices of the Peace.

The Third, of the Diviſions and Sub-diviſions contained in the Appendix: And, **The Fourth,** of The Principal Matters.

And **The Precedents** Tranſlated into *Engliſh.*

ALSO

ADDENDA, containing

The Statutes of 16, 17, 18 & 19 *Geo.* II. with all the Modern Caſes of Authority publiſhed ſince the Year 1742, down to the Preſent Time.

Juſtice is the Staff of Peace, and the Maintenance of Honour. Cic.

In the SAVOY:

Printed by HENRY LINTOT (Aſſignee of *Edw. Sayer,* Eſq;) and Sold by **S. Birt,** at the *Bible* and *Ball* in *Ave-Mary-Lane*; **D. Browne,** at the *Black Swan* without *Temple-Bar*; and **J. Shuckburgh,** at the *Sun* next the *Inner Temple-Gate* in *Fleetſtreet.* M.DCC.XLVI.

Title page of *The Country Justice,* by Michael Dalton, 1618.

Dom. 1612, before Sir James Altham, and Sir Edw. Beverly Judges of Assise there.

These Witches have ordinarily a familiar, or spirit, which appeareth to them.

Their said familiar hath some bigg or little teat upon their body and in some secret place, where he sucketh them.

They have often pictures of Clay, or Waxe (like a man, &c.) found in their house.

If the dead body bleed, upon the Witches touching it.

The testimony of the person hurt, upon his death.

The examination and confession of the children, or servants of the Witch.

Their owne voluntarie confession, which exceedes all other evidence.

Dalton's *Country Justice* was not superseded until 1755 in England. However, in 1736, a Virginia justice named Webb published an updated handbook, *The Office and Authority of a Justice of Peace.*

THE ACT OF 1736

The Witchcraft Statute of James I was repealed in 1736, after minimal opposition, and replaced by the Act of 1736. The new statute removed witchcraft as a felony but retained the punishment of a year's imprisonment and public repentance for "persons pretending to use witchcraft, tell fortunes or discover stolen goods by skill in the occult sciences." The Act of 1736 remained in force until 1951.

THE OFFICE AND AUTHORITY OF A JUSTICE OF PEACE

In 1736, George Webb, a justice of the peace in New Kent County, published *The Office and Authority of a Justice of Peace.* Printed in Williamsburg, it was known within the colony as "Webb's *Justice.*" Webb's book was a compilation and summary of "the Common and Statute Laws of England, and Acts of Assembly, now in Force: And adapted to the Constitution and Practice of Virginia." The book was intended to replace Dalton's *The Country Justice,* of 1618.

On the subject of witchcraft, Webb wrote:

> *The Existence of Witches, or Persons of either Sex, who have real Correspondence and familiar Conversation with Evil Spirits, has been a Subject of controversy among learned Men; And latter Ages have produced very few Instances of Convictions of Witchcraft: But nevertheless, 'tis a Capital Offence.*

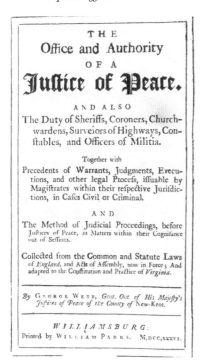

Title page of Webb's *Office and Authority of a Justice of the Peace,* 1736.

Not yet reflecting the new Witchcraft Act of 1736, Webb's book went on to list the actual offenses of witchcraft, noting that certain of these crimes were felonies, while others were merely punishable by one year's imprisonment without bail. The convicted witch had to stand in the pillory every quarter of that year and publicly confess his or her offense. He concluded with this advice:

> *Information of Witchcraft ought not to be received by Justices of Peace, nor Prosecution awarded thereupon, without strong and apparent Cause, proved by sufficient Witnesses, upon Oath: If Process is found necessary, the Proceedings must be as in other Capital Offences.*

Despite the decriminalization of witchcraft and the decline in prosecutions after 1736, many educated and respected people remained steadfast in their beliefs. In 1775, the noted legal expert William Blackstone wrote:

> *To deny the possibility, nay, actual existence of witchcraft and sorcery, is at once flatly to contradict the revealed word of God, in various passages both of the old and new testament· and the thing itself is a truth to which every nation in the world hath in its turn borne testimony, either by examples seemingly well attested, or by prohibitory laws; which at least suppose the possibility of a commerce with evil spirits.*

Benefit of Clergy

In colonial Virginia, the General Court at Jamestown, and later in Williamsburg, was the only tribunal in the colony that could impose a death sentence against a free defendant. A felon convicted by the General Court and sentenced to execution could, in some cases, escape his fate by pleading "benefit of clergy."

Dating from the Middle Ages, this legal privilege of escape could be granted by the court to any prisoner who could demonstrate an ability to read a passage from the Bible. In England, the Psalm 51 was commonly used. Upon successfully reading the prescribed passage ("O God, have mercy upon me, according to thine heartfelt mercifulness"), a condemned felon would be branded and then released. A repeat criminal could claim the benefit of clergy only once.

Before 1732, the privilege was normally extended only to white males. After that date, women, "negroes, mulattoes and Indians were legally allowed to ask for consideration, although there are instances of it being allowed in cases prior to 1732.

The benefit of clergy could not be given to a felon whose crime was willful murder, rape, treason, arson, horse stealing, burglary or robbery. Beginning with Henry VIII's Act of 1542, witchcraft was also considered a crime "without benefit of clergy."

EXECUTIONS

Often part of modern popular thought about witchcraft is the idea that witches were burned at the stake for their crimes. In reality, burning was the definitive legal punishment only on the European continent and in Scotland. This was because these regions identified witchcraft with heresy, which was defined as an opinion or doctrine at variance with the orthodox or accepted doctrine of the church. The punishment for heresy was burning.

In actual practice, burning someone as a punishment was mostly symbolic because the condemned would usually be strangled or stabbed to death before the actual burning. In extreme cases, especially in Germany, torture and mutilation might occur before burning.

Left: A Dutch heretic witch being executed by burning. Copper etching by Jan Luyken, 1685.

Below: Contemporary engraving of witches being hanged in England. *Wikimedia Commons.*

In England and its colonies however, witchcraft was not seen to be the same as heresy. Although religious thought regarding the devil was involved, the results of the crime of witchcraft came under the nature of felonious murder or destruction of property. The proper English (and Virginian) punishment for a felony was death by hanging. Although there were legal burnings in England, these were for heretical religious thought and not for harm or destruction caused by witchcraft.

III

THE EXPERTS

Being a Brief Description of What the Noted Authorities on Witchcraft Had to Say

The fearefull abounding at this time in this countrie, of these detestable slaves of the Devill, the Witches or enchanters, hath moved me... so farre as I can, to resolve the doubting harts of many; both that such assaultes of Sathan are most certainly practized, and that the instrumentes thereof, merits most severely to be punished...
—*James VI of Scotland,* Daemonologie, *1596*

The existence of witches was generally not doubted by the average Englishman, and hence the average Virginian, in the seventeenth and early eighteenth century. What counted as evidence of witchcraft, however, was a matter of debate. The Witchcraft Act of 1604 clearly stated, and King James I clearly believed, that witchcraft was practiced by anyone who used "any Invocation or Conjuration of any evill and spirit, or shall consult covenant with entertaine employ feede or rewarde any evill and wicked Spirit to or for any intent or purpose."

At the same time, however, Anglican clergyman and academic Samuel Harsnett wrote:

> *They that have their brains baited and their fancies distempered with the imaginations and apprehensions of Witches, Conjurors, and Fairies and all that Lymphatical Chimera, I find to be marshalled in one of these five ranks: Children, Fools, Women, Cowards, sick or black melancholic discomposed wits.*

Since the charge of witchcraft could bring a sentence of death, there was a great concern among those conducting witchcraft examinations that no mistakes be made in the true discovery of a witch. Fortunately for the largely untrained justices who sat in the courts of colonial Virginia, there was a wealth of reference material available regarding proper proof. For centuries, learned scholars had written and discussed the correct way to discover witches. In response, there were also critics of "witch finding." The gentleman justices of Virginia could consult a number of authorities.

MALLEUS MALEFICARUM

Written by two Dominican friars, Heinrich Kramer and Jakob Sprenger, *Malleus Maleficarum* (*The Hammer of Witches*) was one of the earliest and most influential books ever published on witchcraft. Published in Latin in 1487, it became the definitive work on how to discover and punish witches. It endorsed torture to obtain confessions and promoted the extermination of witches. Describing witches as heretics, it specified burning as the only acceptable method of execution. *Malleus Maleficarum* was intended to justify the accepted church doctrine toward witches with theological references and offer methods of detection and examination. It established many of the delusions and fears concerning witches and soon came to function as a guide for church inquisitors.

Title page of *Malleus Maleficarum*. This Catholic treatise, first published in 1487, was the best known and most detailed discourse on witchcraft. *Public domain.*

The work was published thirteen times between 1487 and 1520 and another sixteen times between 1574 and 1669. Although popular throughout Europe, the first English translation was not printed until 1584. Records indicate that it was consulted and referred to, but its impact in Anglican English courts was weakened by the fact that it was a Catholic treatise. Unfortunately, King James I plagiarized passages from the *Malleus* in his own work *Daemonologie*. Both the *Malleus* and King James's work were known and available to educated Virginians in the colonial period.

THE DISCOVERY OF WITCHCRAFT

Reginald Scot was a gentleman from a leading family in southeastern England. He had attended Oxford University and served as a justice of the peace and member of Parliament. In his book *The Discovery of Witchcraft*, published in England in 1584, Scot warned that learned men and justices of the peace should exercise common sense and caution during witchcraft examinations.

Having experience in witchcraft examinations, he contended that there was no supernatural power exercised by either humans or demons. His opinion was that only God possessed the power. Furthermore, Scot asserted that witchcraft was only an illusion only accomplished by conjurer's tricks or the "cozening art."

In his book, he intended to prove:

> *The common opinions of Witches contracting with Divels, Spirits, or Familiars; and their power to kill, torment, and consume the bodies of men women, and children, or other creatures by diseases or otherwise; their flying in the Air, &c. To be but imaginary Erronious conceptions and novelties…*

He detailed how mountebanks and conjurors could fool people with simple tricks and that many of the so-called witches were actually only harmless old women. A voice of reason at the time, Scot declared:

> *And because it may appeare unto the world what treacherous and faithless dealing, what extreame and intolerable tyranie, what grosse and fond absurdities, what unaturall and uncivil discourtesie, what cancred and spiteful malice, what outrageous and barbarous crueltie, what lewd and false packing, what cunning and craftie intercepting, what bald and peevish interpretations, what abominable and devilish inventions, and what flat and plain knaveries is practiced against these old women; I will set downe the whole order of the inquisition, to the everlasting, inexcusable, and apparent shame of all witchmongers.*

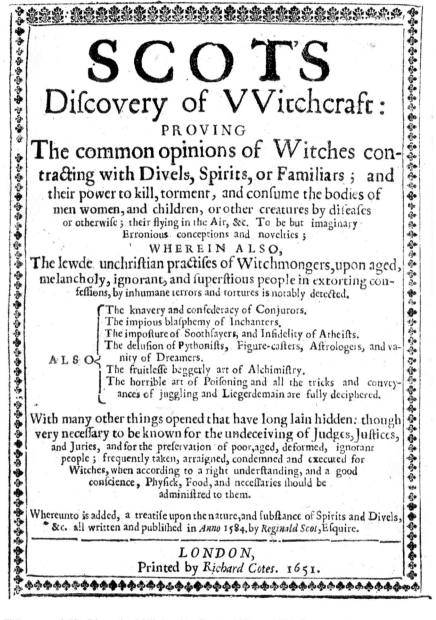

SCOTS

Difcovery of VVitchcraft:

PROVING

The common opinions of Witches con-
tracting with Divels, Spirits, or Familiars ; and
their power to kill, torment, and confume the bodies of
men women, and children, or other creatures by difeafes
or otherwife ; their flying in the Air, &c. To be but imaginary
Erronious conceptions and novelties ;

WHEREIN ALSO,

The lewde unchriftian practifes of Witchmongers, upon aged,
melancholy, ignorant, and fuperftious people in extorting con-
feffions, by inhumane terrors and tortures is notably detected.

ALSO
- The knavery and confederacy of Conjurors.
- The impious blafphemy of Inchanters.
- The impofture of Soothfayers, and Infidelity of Atheifts.
- The delufion of Pythonifts, Figure-cafters, Aftrologers, and va-
nity of Dreamers.
- The fruitleffe beggerly art of Alchimiftry.
- The horrible art of Poifoning and all the tricks and convcy-
ances of juggling and Liegerdemain are fully deciphered.

With many other things opened that have long lain hidden: though
very neceffary to be known for the undeceiving of Judges, Juftices,
and Juries, and for the prefervation of poor, aged, deformed, ignorant
people ; frequently taken, arraigned, condemned and executed for
Witches, when according to a right underftanding, and a good
confcience, Phyfick, Food, and neceffaries fhould be
adminiftred to them.

Whereunto is added, a treatife upon the nature, and fubftance of Spirits and Divels,
&c. all written and publifhed in *Anno* 1584. by *Reginald Scot*, Efquire.

LONDON,
Printed by *Richard Cotes.* 1651.

Title page of *The Discoverie of Witchcraft* by Reginald Scot, 1584. It was written to counter
the idea of witches and to explain that real witchcraft did not exist. *Public domain.*

King James VI of Scotland countered Scot's assertions in his own book, *Daemonologie*, published in 1597. When he later became king of England in 1603, he ordered that all copies of Scot's book were to be burned. The work survived, however, as a testament against the persecutions of the time.

DAEMONOLOGIE

In 1597, King James VI published a book titled *Daemonologie*, which he had personally handwritten as a refutation of Reginald Scot's *The Discovery of Witchcraft*. In the preface, he referred to witches as "these detestable slaves of the Devill." It was not necessarily an original piece of scholarship in that he revised and rephrased parts of the earlier Catholic work *Malleus Maleficarum*. Interestingly, while the *Malleus Maleficarum* was not specifically used by English authorities, King James's version enjoyed great favor, especially after being republished in London in 1603, the year he came to the English throne.

Written as a fictional, philosophical dialogue between two scholars, *Daemonologie* put forth the creed that witches and witchcraft truly existed and that authorities should hunt and prosecute all the earthly followers of Satan. In the chapter on "the tryall and punishment of witches," two scholars, Philomathes and Epistemon, discuss the proper punishment for witchcraft:

> PHILOMATHES: *Then to make an ende of our conference, since I see it drawes late, what forme of punishment thinke ye merites these Magicians and Witches? for I see that ye account them to be all alike guiltie?*
>
> EPISTEMON: *They ought to be put to death according to the Law of God, the civill and imperial law, and municipall law of all Christian nations.*
>
> PHILOMATHES: *But what kinde of death, I pray you?*
>
> EPISTEMON: *It is commonly used by fire, but that is an indifferent thing to be used in every cuntrie, according to the Law or custome thereof.*
>
> PHILOMATHES: *But ought no sexe, age nor ranck to be exempted?*
>
> EPISTEMON: *None at all (being so used by the lawful Magistrate) for it is the highest poynt of Idolatrie, wherein no exception is admitted by the law of God.*

DÆMONOLOGIE,

IN FORME
OF A DIA-
LOGVE,

Diuided into three books:

WRITTEN BY THE HIGH
and mightie Prince, I A M E S by the
grace of God King of England,
Scotland, France *and* Ireland,
Defender of the Faith, &c.

LONDON,
Printed by *Arnold Hatfield* for
Robert VVald-graue.
1 6 0 3

Title page of
Dæmonologie *by*
King James VI of
Scotland, later King
James I of England.
Public domain.

When he came to the throne of England in 1603, James's ideas on witchcraft and the supernatural came with him, just in time to influence the early English settlers in Virginia. Copies of *Daemonologie* are listed in the inventories of early Virginian's private libraries.

THE KING JAMES BIBLE

In 1604, the same year that the witchcraft statutes of King James I were enacted, the king also authorized a commission of scholars to review all known biblical texts and create a new and "uncorrupt" translation of the Bible. Published in 1611, the new King James Bible became the accepted Holy Writ for the Church of England. Colonial Virginians embraced it along with the Book of Common Prayer as they attended their parish churches.

Two verses in particular that specifically mentioned the word *witch* were used as proof of God's disapproval of witches:

> *Exodus 22:18*
> *Thou shall not suffer a witch to live.*

> *Deuteronomy 18:10*
> *There shall not be found among you any one that maketh his son or his daughter to pass through fire, or that useth divination, or an observer of times, or an enchanter, or a witch.*

A third verse referring to witches was also often cited:

> *Leviticus 20:27*
> *A man also or woman that hath a familiar spirit, or that is a wizard, shall surely be put to death: they shall stone them with stones: their blood shall be upon them.*

Authorities in colonial Virginia were never as rabid in their prosecution of accused witches as were their counterparts in puritanical Massachusetts. The historical records suggest very little ecclesiastical influence in the surviving cases, but by the mid-eighteenth century, the religious revival known as the Great Awakening had swept across the colonies and its effects were strongly felt in Virginia. Beginning in the 1740s, "enthusiastical" Presbyterians, Methodists and Baptists were shaking up the established church in the colony. Evangelical preachers such as Samuel Davies, William Robinson and George Whitefield influenced many Virginians.

Although most people's belief in witchcraft had fallen by the wayside before the Awakening occurred, there were holdouts among the Presbyterian and Methodist congregations in Virginia that still felt

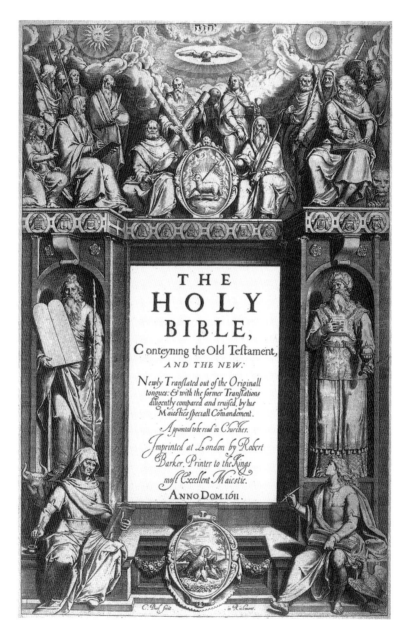

Title page of King James Version Bible from 1611. *Wikimedia Commons.*

threatened by Satan's disciples. In 1768, John Wesley, the founder of Methodism, wrote:

> *The English in general, and indeed most of the men of learning in Europe, have given up all accounts of witches and apparitions as mere old wives fables. I am sorry for it, and I willingly take this opportunity of entering my solemn protest against this violent compliment which so many that believe in the Bible pay to those who do not believe it.... [T]he giving up of witchcraft is in effect giving up the Bible.*

DISCOURSE OF THE DAMNED ART OF WITCHCRAFT

The Puritan preacher William Perkins was a prolific writer who included among his works sermons on witchcraft. His book *Discourse of the Damned Art of Witchcraft*, published posthumously in 1608 and reprinted in a second edition in 1610, supported the ideas expressed by King James I in his book *Daemonologie*.

Perkins's views were a reasoned defense of the belief in witchcraft, although he did not ascribe to the use of superstitious tests, such as "ducking" or "swimming" an accused witch. He held that witchcraft accusations should be entered into with common sense and rational examination. If guilt was established, however, Perkins stated, "all Witches being thoroughly convicted by the Magistrate, ought according to the Law of Moses to be put to death."

In 1692, the Boston minister Cotton Mather listed a synopsis of "Mr. Perkins' way for the discovery of witches" in his book *The Wonders of the Invisible World*:

> *There are Presumptions, which do at least probably and conjecturally note one to be a Witch. These give occasion to examine, yet they are no sufficient Causes of Conviction.*

> *If any Man or Woman be notoriously defamed for a Witch this yields a strong Suspition. Yet the Judge ought carefully to look, that the Report be made by Men of Honesty and Credit.*

Left: English cleric and theologian William Perkins, painted by an unknown artist, 1602. *Wikimedia Commons.*

Right: Mezzotint portrait of Cotton Mather, circa 1700. *Public domain.*

If a Fellow-Witch, or Magician, give Testimony of any Person to be Witch; this indeed is not sufficient for Condemnation; but it is a fit Presumption to cause a strait Examination.

If after Cursing there follow Death, or at least some mischief: for Witches are wont to practise their mischievous Facts by Cursing and Banning: This also is a sufficient matter of Examination, tho' not of Conviction.

If after Enmity, Quarreling, or Threatening, a present mischief does follow; that also is a great Presumption.

If the Party suspected be the Son or Daughter, the man-servant or maid-servant, the Familiar Friend, near Neighbor, or old Companion, of a known and convicted witch; this may be likewise a Presumption; for Witchcraft is an Art that may be learned, and conveyed from man to man.

Some add this for a Presumption: If the Party suspected be found to have the Devil's mark; for it is commonly thought, when the Devil makes a Covenant with them, he alwaies leaves his mark behind them, whereby he knows them for his own: a mark whereof no evident Reason in Nature can be given.

Lastly, If the party examined be Unconstant, or contrary to himself, in his deliberate Answers, it argueth a Guilty Conscience, which stops the freedom of Utterance. And yet there are causes of astonishment, which may befall the Good, as well as the Bad.

But then there is a Conviction, discovering the Witch, which must proceed from just and sufficient proofs, and not from bare presumptions.

Scratching of the suspected party, and Recovery thereupon, with several other such weak Proofs; as also, the fleeting of the suspected Party, thrown upon the Water; these proofs are so far from being sufficient, that some of them are, after a sort, practices of witchcraft.

The Testimony of some Wizzard, tho' offering to shew the Witches Face in a Glass: This, I grant, may be a good Presumption, to cause a strait Examination; but a sufficient Proof of Conviction it cannot be. If the Devil tell the Grand jury, that the person in question is a Witch, and offers withal to confirm the same by Oath, should the inquest receive his Oath or Accusation to condemn the man? Assuredly no. And yet, that is as much as the Testimony of another Wizzard, who only by the Devil's help reveals the Witch.

If a man, being dangerously sick, and like to dye, upon Suspicion, will take it on his Death, that such a one hath bewitched him, it is an Allegation of the same nature, which may move the Judge to examine the Party, but it is of no moment for Conviction.

Among the sufficient means of Conviction, the first is, the free and voluntary Confession of the Crime, made by the party suspected and accused, after Examination. I say not, that a bare confession is sufficient, but a Confession after due Examination, taken upon pregnant presumptions. What needs now more witness or further Enquiry?

There is a second sufficient Conviction, by the Testimony of two Witnesses, of good and honest Report, avouching before the Magistrate, upon their own Knowledge, these two things: either that the party accused hath made a League with the Devil, or hath done some known practice of witchcraft. And, all Arguments that do necessarily prove either of these, being brought by two sufficient Witnesses, are of force fully to convince the party suspected.

If it can be proved, that the party suspected hath called upon the Devil, or desired his Help, this is pregnant proof of a League formerly made between them.

If it can be proved, that the party hath entertained a Familiar Spirit, and had Conference with it, in the likeness of some visible Creatures; here is Evidence of witchcraft.

If the witnesses affirm upon Oath that the suspected person hath done any action or work which necessarily infers a Covenant made, as, that he hath used Enchantments, divined things before they come to pass, and that peremptorily, raised Tempests, caused the Form of a dead man to appear; it proveth sufficiently, that he or she is a Witch.

Educated Virginians of the colonial period were familiar with Perkins's writings. In 1621, a three-volume set of Perkins's works had been dispatched to Virginia, and eighteenth-century inventories of private libraries reveal copies of his works. In 1744, for example, Colonel William Byrd II possessed a copy of Perkins's *Art of Witchcraft*.

THE DISPLAYING OF SUPPOSED WITCHCRAFT

John Webster made an important contribution to the literature concerning witchcraft with his book *The Displaying of Supposed Witchcraft*. With the coming of the Age of Reason, in which men began to look at the world around them with a scientific eye, Webster presented the idea that evidence of witchcraft should be subjected to the same scientific examination. Webster did not deny witchcraft existed. However, he felt that there was not the need to blame the devil for every misfortune. In his introduction, Webster stated:

[I]t is discretion to bear that patiently for which humane prudence can find no remedy. Others…who are grown obstinate in their minds and wills, concerning Spirits, Apparitions, Witchcraft, Sorcery, Inchantment, and the like, and are grown pertinacious and resolute to stick to and hold those opinions that they have imbibed through ignorant education: not considering that perseverance in a good cause, and well-grounded opinion is laudable and commendable, but perniciousness in a bad and ill grounded tenant, is

THE

DISPLAYING

OF SUPPOSED

WITCHCRAFT.

Wherein is affirmed that there are many forts of

Deceivers and Impostors,

AND

Divers perfons under a paffive *Delufion* of

MELANCHOLY and *FANCY*.

But that there is a *Corporeal League* made betwixt the
DEVIL and the WITCH,

Or that he fucks on the *Witches Body*, has *Carnal Copulation*, or
that *Witches* are turned into *Cats*, *Dogs*, raife Tempefts, or
the like, is utterly denied and difproved.

Wherein alfo is handled,

The Exiftence of Angels and Spirits, the truth of Apparitions, the Nature of
Aftral and Sydereal Spirits, the force of Charms, and Philters;
with other abftrufe matters.

By *John Webfter*, Practitioner in Phyfick.

*Falfa etenim opiniones Hominum praeoccupantes, non folùm furdas, fed & cæcos faciunt, itá ut
videre nequeant, quæ aliis perfpicua apparent.* Galen. lib. 8. de Comp. Med.

LONDON,

Printed by *J. M.* and are to be fold by the Bookfellers in *London.* 1677.

Title page of *The Displaying of
Supposed Witchcraft*, 1677, by
John Webster. *Public domain.*

as bad and hurtful. And it is every wise mans duty to study the cultivation
and improvement of the goods of the mind, and never to be ashamed to
learn that of which they were ignorant before. For the minds of men are not
only darkned in the fall of Adam, but also much misled, by the sucking in
of errors in their younger and more unwary years, from whence they ought
to endeavour with might and main to extricate and deliver themselves. But
he that is wilfully setled upon the lees and dregs of former opinions, though
never so erroneous, hath shut forth all further light from shining into his
understanding, and so is become willfully blind. To such as these we shall
only propose the example and practice of the Apostle, who saith: When I
was a child, I spake as a child, I understood as a child, I thought as a child:
But when I became a man, I put away childish things.

Published in London in 1677, Webster's book and views were known in Virginia, as is evidenced by a copy that resided in the chamber of Virginia's governor's council. Ralph Wormeley, president of the council and acting governor of the colony for a short time in 1698, possessed his own volume of Webster's book. Upon his death in 1701, an inventory of Wormeley's library lists a copy of *The Displaying of Supposed Witchcraft*.

SADUCIMUS TRIUMPHATUS

Even with the enlightened views of men such as John Webster, traditional views persisted. Joseph Glanville, the rector of Bath Abbey and a fellow of the Royal Society, wrote *Philosophical Considerations Touching Witches and Witchcraft* in 1666. Running through several editions, his work was republished posthumously in 1681 as *Saducimus Triumphatus; Or, Full and Plain Evidence Concerning Witches and Apparitions*.

Glanville felt that witches and witchcraft proved the existence of Satan and to deny them was close to denying the existence of God. He attempted to provide answers to objections of supernatural beliefs. In his work, he listed the attributes of witches, such as the ability to fly to remote places,

Woodcut of the devil tempting nuns. From *Saducimus Triumphatus*, 1681.

transform into animals and the raising of tempests or storms, all of which were common notions in colonial Virginia.

In 1733, a court-ordered inventory and appraisement of the personal estate of "Robert Beverly, Esq., deceased," of Spotsylvania County, lists a copy of Glanville's *Saducimus Triumphatus*.

IV

THE WITCHES

Being a Brief Description of Those Poor, Wretched
Souls Accused of the Crime of Witchcraft in the
Colony of Virginia and Its Vicinage

*[E]verie such Offendor or Offendors, theire Ayders Abettors and Counsellors, being
of the saide Offences dulie and lawfullie convicted and attainted, shall suffer
pains of deathe as a Felon or Felons.*
—*Witchcraft Act of James I, 1604*

When the first English settlers arrived in Virginia and settled at Jamestown in
1607, they brought with them their belief in witchcraft and the supernatural.
They were largely influenced by their king, an ardent believer who had
published his views in his book *Daemonologie*.

NATIVE AMERICANS

It is not surprising that when these first settlers met the Native American
inhabitants of Virginia, they immediately looked upon them as barbarians
who worshiped idols and were under the influence of Satan. At that time,
in the Chesapeake Bay region of Virginia, there were approximately fifteen
thousand Algonquian Indians living in the area between the Potomac River
and the modern North Carolina border. They were mostly members of, or
allied with, what was called the Powhatan Confederacy, under the chief
werowance or leader, Chief Powhatan.

An Algonquian warrior of Virginia from a Theodor De Bry woodcut, from a painting by John White. *Wikimedia Commons.*

The Powhatan Indians worshiped many spirits, chief of which was Okee. This particular spirit was supposedly very ugly and required sacrifices of tobacco, blood, deer fat and so forth. One account stated that Okee ruled the underworld and would bring famine, drought and disease if angered. Guided by shamans or medicine men called *kwiocosuk*, the Powhatans frequently sought Okee's approval on decisions and actions, and his effigy was brought into battle at least once. Understandably, because of their religious indoctrination, evidence of any non-Christian deity or activities made the English believe that the Indians were servants of Satan.

When he first met Chief Powhatan, Captain Smith described him as "more like a devill than a man."

In 1612, the English theologian Reverend Alexander Whitaker wrote from Virginia that

> *in a march upp Nansemond River as our men passed by one of their Townes, there yssued out on the shoare a mad crewe dauncing like Anticks, or our Morris dancers before whom there were Quiokosite (or theire Priest) tossed smoke and flame out of a thinge like a censer. An Indian (by the name of Memchumps) amongst our men seeing this dance tould us that there would be very much raine presently and indeed there was a forthwith exceeding thunder and lighteninge and much raine within 5 miles and so further of.... All which things make me think that there be great witches amongst them and they very familiar with the divill.*

Conspicuous in Whitaker's remarks is the association of a symbol of Catholicism, a censer, with witchcraft and the devil. Whitaker went on to write in a sermon published as *Good Newes from Virginia*:

Algonquin Indians dancing, by Theodor De Bry, 1590. *Public domain.*

Their priests (whom they call Quiokosoughs) are no other but such as our English Witches are. They live naked in bodie, as if their shame of their sinne deserved no covering: Their names areas naked as their bodie: they esteeme it as a virtue to lie, deceive, and steale as their master the divell teacheth them.

Later in his sermon, Whitaker declared that the Indian priests belonged to "a generation of vipers even of Sathans owne brood."

In 1613, William Crashaw wrote of Virginia that "Satan visibly and palpably raignes there, more than any other known place of the world." Master George Percy described the first Indians he encountered in Virginia as "so many wolves or Devils." Regardless of the opinions of the earliest settlers in Virginia, there are no known records of any arrest, detention or prosecution of any Virginia Native Americans for the crime of witchcraft.

FINDING WITCHES AMONG THEMSELVES

Beginning in the mid-1620s, as the Virginia colony grew with new arrivals, the English settlers began to find disciples of the devil in their own communities. The first recorded witchcraft inquiry in Virginia dates to 1626. From then until the early eighteenth century, the colony's surviving records indicate several witchcraft investigations, petitions, slander suits and countersuits.

There seem to have been only a few instances or mention of witchcraft between 1626 and 1641. Oddly enough, there is no indication of any cases during the period of the first English Civil War (1642–46), when witch mania flourished in England.

It was led by the supposed "Witchfinder General," Matthew Hopkins, a zealous Puritan, who fervently sought out witches in East Anglia until he retired due to ill health in 1647. During that time, however, he and his supporters were responsible for as many as three hundred executions in England.

Beginning in the 1650s, witchcraft began to appear once more in Virginia legal records and continued until 1706. After that, there is only one known instance of a witchcraft proceeding, in 1730, before the law changes in 1736.

In the American colonies as a whole, men, women, children and even animals were accused of witchcraft, but the great majority of victims were female. In Europe, it is noted

Matthew Hopkins, the celebrated English witchfinder. *Wikimedia Commons.*

that on average, 80 percent of suspected witches and 85 percent of executed witches were women. Today, there are many opinions and explanations of this, including questions of temperament, age, property, class and sexual tension. At the time, the Puritan preacher William Perkins wrote:

> *The woman being the weaker sexe, is sooner entangled by the devill's illusions, with the damnable art, than the man. And in all ages it is found true by experience, that the devil hath more easily and oftener prevailed with women than with men.... [H]is first temptation in the beginning, was with Eve a woman, and since he pursueth his practice accordingly as making for his advantage. For where he findeth easiest entrance, and best entertainment, thither will he oftenest resort.*

What follows is a chronological listing of those accused of witchcraft in colonial Virginia between 1626 and 1730.

1626—JOAN WRIGHT

Joan Wright, a midwife, and her husband, Robert, a sawyer, were among the earliest settlers in Virginia, termed "ancient planters." They had arrived separately in 1609 and married in 1610. Early on, Joan ran afoul of the colony's drastic *Lawes Divine, Moral and Martial* and was whipped for improperly hemming a shirt. By 1625, they were listed as living with two children in the household of Anthony Bonall, a French silk maker and wine grape cultivator in Elizabeth City County. By this time, Robert had accrued several debts and was being dogged by creditors. Joan was known as a "cunning woman" who supposedly possessed clairvoyant powers.

Woodcut of a cunning woman. From *The Wonderful Discoverie of Elizabeth Sawyer a Witch*, 1621.

By 1626, the Wrights had moved to Pace's Paines, west of Gray's Creek, across the James River from Jamestown in what would become Surry County. It was there that she was formally accused of being a witch and examined by the local justices, who determined that there was enough evidence against her. Accordingly, she was brought before the General Court at Jamestown to be heard and judged. The governor of the colony, Sir George Yeardley, presided as chief justice along with members of his council, Captain Francis West and Dr. John Potts, to determine if the accusations were true.

Through surviving records, we can assume that the witnesses heard were also those who had testified against Goodwife Wright before the local magistrates. The first witness against Mrs. Wright was Lieutenant Giles Allington, who stated:

> *Liut. Gieles Allington sworne and examined sayeth, That he harde Sargeant Booth saye that he was croste by a woman and for a twelve months space he havinge very fayre game to shute at, yet he could never kill any thinge but this deponent cannot say that it was good wiefe Wright. Fourther this deponent sayeth, that he had spoken to good wiefe Wrighte for to bringe his wiefe to bed, but the saide goodwief beinge left handed, his wiefe desired him to get Mrs. Grave to be her midwiefe, which this deponent did.*

As stated in Allington's testimony, Joan Wright was left-handed, which was considered "different" or unlucky. Traditionally, the left side, and therefore left-handedness being bad, is very old. Ancient Babylonians deemed the left side bad and the right side good. Homer spoke of birds flying to the right as a good omen, while those flying to the left was unfavorable. The Latin word *sinistra* meant "left" but eventually took on a meaning of "evil" or "unlucky." This survives in the English word *sinister*.

The idea of a left-handed midwife at her child's birthing upset Allington's wife to such an extent that she made her husband retain the services of the second midwife, a Mrs. Grave. This apparently brought misfortune to Lieutenant Allington and his family. His statement continues:

> [T]*he next daye after his wiefe was delivered, the saide goodwiefe Wright went awaye from his howse very much discontented, in regarde the other midwiefe had brought his wiefe to bedd, shortlie after this, this deponents wiefes brest grew dangerouslie sore of an Imposture and was a moneth or 5 weeks before she was recovered, Att which tyme This deponent him selfe fell sick and contynued the space of three weeks, And further sayeth that his childe after it was borne fell sick and soe contynued the space of two moneths, and afterwards recovered, And so did Contynue well for the space of a moneth, And afterwards fell into extreeme payne the space of five weeks and so departed.*

Under the law, this evidence, causing pain, sickness and the death of a child, was more than enough to convict Mrs. Wright of a felony, if it could be proved.

The next witness, Rebecca Graye, told how Mrs. Wright had predicted that she would soon bury her husband. She went on to testify that a Mr. Felgate and Thomas Harris had also received similar warnings from Goodwife Wright concerning their respective spouses:

> *Rebecka Graye sworne and examined sayeth That good wief Wright did tell her this deponent That by one Token which this deponent had in her forehed she should burye her Husbande, And fourther sayeth that good wiefe Wright did tell this deponent that she told Mr ffellgate he should bury his wiefe (which cam to pass) And further this deponent sayeth that goodwiefe Wright did tell this deponent, That she tolde Thomas Harris he should burie his first wiefe being then bethrothed unto him (which cam so to pass) further this deponent sayeth that goodwiefe Wright did tell her that there*

was a woman said to her (I have a cross man to my husband) To whom good wiefe Wright replide (be content) for thow shalte shortlie burie him (which cam so to pass).

According to the witnesses, Mrs. Wright seemed to be very good at foretelling death, even foretelling the death of hens:

Daniell Watkins sworned and examined sayeth that about february last past, this deponent beinge at Mr Perryes Plantatione Ther was Robert Thresher who had a cowple of henns pourposinge to send them over to Elzabeth Arundle And good wiefe Wright beinge there in place, saide to Robert Thresher, why do you keepe these henns heere tyed upp, The maide you meane to send them to will be dead before the henns come to her.

Robert Thresher came forth to testify for himself and, along with the statements of Elizabeth Gates, suggested that Mrs. Wright also tended to cause property destruction:

Robert Thresher sworne and examined sayeth yt good wiefe Wright came to him and requested him to give her some plants, He answered yt when he had served his owne tourne, she should have some, so she went away and yt night all his plants were drowned.

Elizabeth Gates sworne and examined sayeth yt Goodwiefe Wright came to Mr. Moores at Kickotan to buy some chickens, but he would sell her none, shortly after the chickens died, and after that the henn died, and this she affirmeth she had hearde from others.

Mrs. Isabell Perry came forward to tell the court how Mrs. Wright had been causing trouble, even before she arrived in Surry County:

Mrs Isabell Perry sworned and examined sayeth that uppon the losinge of a logg of light wood owt of the fforte, good wiefe Wrighte rayled uppon a girl of good wiefe gates for stealing of the same, wheruppon good wiefe gates Charged the said good wiefe Wright with witchcrafte, And said that she had done many bad things at Kickotan.

Apparently, Mrs. Perry had spoken openly to Joan, asking why she would allow herself to be spoken of as a witch:

[T]his Examinate Chid the saide Good wiefe Wright, And said unto her, yf thow knowst thyselfe Cleare of what she Charged thee, why dost thow not complaine And cleare thyselfe of the same, To whom good wiefe Wright replied, god forgive them, and so made light of it, And the said good wiefe Wright Threatened good wiefe Gates girle and told her, that yf she did nott bringe the light wood againe she would make her daunce starke naked and the next morninge the lightwood was founde in the forte.

Mrs. Perry went on to state how Dorothy Bethlehem had questioned why she would allow Joan into her house, Wright being a witch. Mrs. Bethlehem had then revealed to her that Joan had been a witch at Hull in England before coming to Virginia. Her statement read:

Dorethie Behethlem asked this Examint why she did suffer good wiefe to be at her howse, saying she was a very bad woman, and was Accompted a witch amoungst all them at Kickotan

And fourther this deponent [sayeth] *that good wiefe did tell her that when she lived at hull, beinge one day Chirninge of butter there cam a woman to the howse who was accompted for a witch, whereuppon she by directions from her dame Clapt the Chirne staffe to the bottom of the Chirne and clapt her hands across uppon the top of it by which means the witch was not able to stire owt of the place where she was for the space of six howers after which time good wiefe Wright desired her dame to aske the woman why she did not gett her gone, wheruppon the witche fell downe on her knees and asked forgivenes and saide her hande was in the Chirne, and could not stire before her maide lifted upp the staffe of the Chirne, which the saide good wiefe Wright did, and the witch went awaye, but to her perseverance* [perception] *the witch had both her handes at libertie, and this good wiefe Wright affirmeth to be trewe. Fourther Mrs Pery sayeth that good wiefe Wright told her, that she was at Hull her dame beinge sick suspected her selfe to be bewiched, and told good wiefe Wright of it, whereuppon by directione from her dame, That at the cominge of a woman, which was suspected, to take a horshve and flinge it into the oven and when it was red hott, To fflinge it into her dames urine, and so long as the horshve was hott, the witch was sick at the harte, And when the Irone was colde she was well againe, And this good wiefe Wright affirmeth to be trwe alsoe.*

In retrospect, looking at the evidence presented against her, it appears that Joan Wright possessed a personality that irritated everyone and didn't seem to mind being called a witch.

Finally, Joan Wright's husband was brought before the court, where he could only state "that he hath beene married to his wiefe sixteene yeers, but knoweth nothinge by her touching the Crime she is accused of."

Here the records of the General Court's investigation end, and there is no official evidence of any actions taken against Joan Wright. The assumption remains, however, that Joan Wright was probably not found guilty of witchcraft. Even though documents concerning a legal decision don't survive, there are other sources for life in the Virginia colony of 1626, and none of them mentions any punishment or execution of a witch, which certainly would have been big news.

What is known is that in January 1627, Robert petitioned the General Court for permission to be assigned a plot of land on Jamestown Island, possibly to remove his family from so many hostile neighbors. His petition was granted, and he brought his family (presumedly including Joan) to a twelve-acre parcel on the eastern end of Jamestown Island, known as "Labour-In-Vain." Nothing more is known of Joan, but Robert continued to be a debtor, being imprisoned in 1628 and 1629.

1641—Mrs. George Barker

In April 1641, Jane Rookens apparently spoke in anger and called George Barker's wife a witch. It was Jane Rookens, however, who found herself in trouble. The General Court at Jamestown ruled against Mrs. Rookens in a slander suit. Jane's poor husband became the final victim. The court records state:

> *Wheras it appeareth to the court by several depositions that Jane Rookens hath abused and scandalized the wife of George Barker by calling her a witch which the said Rookens doth not remember but denyeth in open court and is sorry for the same offence with which the said Barker was very satisfied, the court hath therefore ordered that William Rookens husband of the said Jane forthwith pay unto the said Barker expenses and charges of court on this behalf sustained.*

Storm at Sea by Willem van de Velde the Younger, 1675. *Wikimedia Commons.*

1654—KATHERINE GRADY

Katherine Grady has the unfortunate distinction of being the only known person who was executed for witchcraft in the colony of Virginia—although, technically, she was not in the colony proper when she met her fate.

In the year 1654, Katherine was a passenger aboard a ship sailing for Virginia. Upon reaching the coast of the colony, the ship rode into a great storm. As it was a common belief that storms at sea were a favorite evil spell cast on travelers by witches, the passengers and crew began to look about for a likely suspect. For whatever reason, poor Katherine Grady seems to have become the object of her fellow passengers' fear and wrath. They convinced the ship's captain, a man named Bennett, that Katherine was the witch who was causing the tempest, to torment her companions. No one knows what sort of evidence was presented by her fellow passengers, but Captain Bennett took matters into his own hands and hanged Katherine, in an effort to end the storm.

Upon reaching port, the captain was called to appear before an admiralty court at Jamestown to answer for his actions. Apparently, Captain Bennett was able to satisfactorily explain his actions and was not detained. The court's exact findings are lost, but the fact remains that although there was no official trial or inquiry into the matter of Katherine Grady's supposed witchcraft, she became a colonial Virginia statistic only because Virginia was Captain Bennett's destination.

1656—WILLIAM HARDING

Poor William Harding was living in Northumberland County on Virginia's Northern Neck when he was accused of witchcraft and sorcery. Reverend David Lindsey of Wicomico Parish brought the accusations before a grand jury of twenty-four freeholders in November 1656. The grand jury accepted several depositions against Harding and decided that some of the accusations were true. The county justices of the peace then deliberated over a proper punishment. Apparently, whatever Harding's witchcraft consisted of, it was not considered to be too life-threatening. The justices ordered that

> *the said Wm. Harding shall forthwith receave ten stripes upon his bare back and forever to be Banished from this County and that hee depart within the space of two moneths And also to pay all the charges of Court.*

In plain English, this meant that although they thought him guilty of witchcraft, the justices didn't bind William Harding over to the General Court in Jamestown but instead ordered him to leave the county after being publicly flogged. In addition, they also gave him two months to leave and wouldn't let him leave until he had paid the costs of his own prosecution. Reading between the lines, it becomes apparent that even though he was found guilty, no one considered Harding a satanic threat to the welfare of the county. For whatever reason, William Harding was not welcome in Northumberland County and someone just wanted him to leave.

This constitutes one of only two known cases of a legal conviction for witchcraft in the Colony of Virginia.

1657—BARBARA WINGBROUGH (WINGBOROUGH)

Barbara Wingbrough appeared before Governor Samuel Matthews and his council sitting as the General Court at Jamestown on December 1, 1657. There, she was "arragned as a witch but acquitted." After the charges were dismissed, the question arose over who should pay the court costs. The governor's council considered the matter but was unable to resolve the matter, turning the question over to the House of Burgesses.

Her accuser was Francis Doughty, who was perhaps influenced by religious zeal. He had been forced to leave England because of his Puritan beliefs and had settled initially in Massachusetts before coming to Virginia. By 1661, he had left Virginia and was residing in the neighboring colony of Maryland, where he accused another woman of witchcraft. Regardless of his religious views, Doughty was described as being prone to "many vices and especially to drinking."

1659—MISTRESS ROBINSON

The justices of the peace in early colonial Virginia appear to have been more skeptical of charges of witchcraft than their New England counterparts. Although their belief in witchcraft and the supernatural was no different from any average Englishman of their time, they took a dim view of false accusations. In 1655, for example, the justices of Lower Norfolk County, meeting at "a private court" at the house of Edward Hall in Lynnhaven, ordered:

> *Whereas divrs dangerous & scandalous speeches have beene raised by some persons concerning sevrall women in this Countie termeing them to be Witches, whereby their reputacons have beene much impaired, and their lives brought in question (for avoydeing the like offence) It is by this Court ordered that what persons soer shall hereafter raise any such like scandal concerninge any partie whatsoever and shall not be able to pvr the same, both upon oath, and by sufficient witness, such person soe offending shall in the first place paie A thousand pounds of tob: and likewise be lyeable to further Censure of the Court.*

In December 1659, the court arraigned Ann Godby for "Slanders & scandals Cast upon Women under the notion of Witches." Several depositions were presented to the court telling how Mrs. Godby had slandered a Mistress Robinson of the county by calling her a witch. Ann's husband, Thomas, was also called forward, as he was responsible under the law for his wife's actions. After hearing all the evidence, the justices decided:

> *Whereas Ann Godby, the wife of Tho. Godby, hath contrary to an order of the court bearing the date of May 1655, concerning some slanders and scandals cast upon women under the notion of witches hath contemptuously acted in abusing and taking the good name and credit of Nico. Robinson's wife, terming her as a witch....It is therefore ordered that the sd Tho. Godby shall pay three hundred pounds of tobo & Caske* fine for her Contempt of the menconed order, [being the first time] *& also pay & defray the Cost of sute together with the Witnesses Charges at twenty Pounds tobo p day als exec.*

Three years later, the House of Burgesses at Jamestown passed "An Act for Punishment of Scandalous Persons," which included a provision to protect husbands from the acts of their wives:

> *Whereas many babbling women slander and scandalize theire neighbors for which their poore husbands are often involved in chargeable and vexatious suits, and cast in great damnages, Be it therefore enacted by the authorities aforesaid that in actions of slander occasioned by the wife after judgment*

An Act for Punishment of scandalous Persons.

Preamble. **I.** WHEREAS many babbling Women slander and scandalize their Neighbours, for which their poor Husbands are often involved in chargeable and vexatious Suits, and cast in great Damages:

In Actions of Slander, occasion'd by the Wife, the Woman to suffer a Ducking for each 500 lb. Tobacco adjudged against the Husband. **II.** BE it therefore Enacted, by the Authority aforesaid, That in Actions of Slander occasioned by the Wife, after Judgment passed for the Damages, the Woman shall be punished by Ducking; and if the Slander be so enormous, as to be adjudged at greater Damages than Five Hundred Pounds of Tobacco, then the Woman to suffer a Ducking for each Five Hundred Pounds of Tobacco adjudged against the Husband, if he refuse to pay the Tobacco.

"An Act for Punishment of Scandalous Persons." From *A Complete Collection of the Laws of VA at a Grand Assembly held at JCC 23 March 1662. Library of Congress.*

passed for the damnages, the woman shall be punished by ducking and if the slander be soe enormous as to be adjudged at greater damnages then five hundred pounds of tobacco then the woman to suffer a ducking for each five hundred pounds of tobacco adjudged against the husband if he refuse to pay the tobacco.

1659—ELIZABETH RICHARDSON

Although not strictly a Virginia matter, the great-grandfather of George Washington was involved as a witness in a witchcraft matter in Maryland in 1659. John Washington of Westmoreland County petitioned a Maryland court to investigate the matter of the execution of Elizabeth Richardson as a witch aboard a merchant ship in the Chesapeake Bay, off Virginia's coast. Captain Edward Prescott of the *Sarah Artch* had allowed his crew to hang Elizabeth, in order to end a storm, which they believed her to have caused,

Exactly how Washington knew the particulars of the affair is unknown, and although he had issued the complaint, Washington failed to attend the court session in Maryland, attending his son's baptism instead. Maryland's governor, Josias Fendall, wrote: "Witnesses examined in Virginia will be of no value here, in this case, for they must be face to face with the party accused or they stand for nothing."

The Maryland court issued a second call for witnesses, but no one appeared and Captain Prescott was released.

1665—ALICE STEPHENS

During the October session of the General Court, Governor Sir William Berkeley and his council examined an accusation of witchcraft against Alice Stephens. The final judgment of the court is unknown although the court clerk recorded the cryptic notation, "Alice Stephens accused as a witch, but not cleared." This meant that Alice should have been bound over to the General Court in Jamestown to be tried as a witch. Whether she was merely punished at a county level under "petite witchcraft" or actually sent to Jamestown is not known, as no further records on her exist.

1668—UNKNOWN WOMAN AND HER CHILDREN

On November 24, 1668, a pardon was requested of the General Court at Jamestown for calling an unnamed woman and her children witches. Again, the surviving records are silent on any acquittal or conviction, but apparently the court was taking seriously the defamation of character caused by slandering someone as a witch.

1671—HANNAH NEAL

Edward Cole of Northumberland County alleged that Hannah, the wife of Captain Christopher Neal, was a witch. Cole and Mrs. Neal had been at odds with each other ever since they had both arrived from England on the same ship.

In 1671, Cole began telling his neighbors how Hannah had foretold that he and his family would never prosper in Virginia. Just as she had predicted, Cole's family and servants soon grew sick and several of his cattle died.

Even though he presented depositions to the county justices, Cole determined to prove by his own devices that Hannah was a witch who had cursed his family. He sent for Hannah to visit his bedridden wife and then nailed an iron horseshoe over the door of his house. Following the logic that a witch could not enter a dwelling so protected, Cole knew that if she hesitated or refused to enter, he would have enough proof of her witchcraft.

Hannah surprised everyone, however, by not only passing promptly into the house but also praying for the sick woman.

Cole, believing in the power of the horseshoe, apologized for his suspicions and stated that his earlier thoughts were "passionately spoken." He agreed to pay all the court costs involved in the suit.

1675—JOAN (JANE) JENKINS

In June 1675, a justice of the peace, sheriff and elected burgess, Captain William Carver, accused Joan Jenkins of Lower Norfolk County of being familiar with evil spirits and using witchcraft. Accordingly, Joan appeared with her husband, Lazarus, at the county court, where Captain Carver made his complaint. Either through the weight of evidence or Captain Carver's influence as a "gentleman" of the county, a special jury of both men and women was impaneled to search the Jenkin's house "according to the 118th chapter of doulton."

Using Michael Dalton's *Country Justice* as its guide, the jury would have looked for "charmes" or "inchantments" and "pictures of Clay or Waxe (like a man)." If the women of the jury went so far as to search Joan's body, they would have looked for a witch's mark or "place upon their bodie" where a familiar would have sought sustenance.

Presumably, they found nothing, for there is no further record of Mrs. Jenkins being bound over for a trial. A revealing side note is the fact that Carver had earlier been involved in a property suit with Joan and Lazarus Jenkins, which possibly led to his accusations.

Carver apparently had a violent temper, especially when he drank. He had several serious quarrels with his neighbors and in 1672 stabbed and killed a dinner companion. Described as behaving irrationally, the General Court found him innocent of murder. It was after this that he had his property dispute with Lazarus Jenkins and subsequently charged Jenkins's wife with witchcraft.

As an epilogue, Captain Carver would meet his end at the gallows the very next year. As a supporter of Nathaniel Bacon's ill-fated rebellion against the authority of Governor Sir William Berkeley, he was captured with others, tried as a rebel and hanged.

1679—ALICE CARTWRITE

In January 1678/9, in Lower Norfolk County, four justices of the peace sat upon an examining court to look into the matter of the death of a member of John Salmon's family.

Salmon maintained that Alice Cartwrite had bewitched his child and caused its death. Such an accusation, if supported by evidence, could lead to the accused being transported to the General Court at Jamestown for trial. If convicted of the use of witchcraft "whereby any person shall be killed," Alice would suffer death.

Whatever evidences were presented to the justices are lost; however, the court fell back on the use of a test to determine if Alice was truly a witch:

> Upon the petition and complaint of Jno. Sammon [sic] against Alice the wife of Thomas Cartwrite concerning the death of a child of the said Sammon who it is supposed was bewitched, it is ordered that the Sheriff do forthwith summon an able jury of women to attend the court tomorrow and search the said Alice according to the direction of the court.

The next day, January 16, a jury of women was formed to examine Alice. There is no record of what the court's precise directions might have been to search her; however, the accepted practice was for the accused to be taken into a separate room, where a private and meticulous physical examination could be made. As outlined by several noted authorities, the jury of women would be searching for witch's marks.

Regardless of how the actual examination took place, the jury, led by forewoman Mary Chichester, delivered their findings to the justices:

> In the diff beetween Jno Salmon plantiff agt Alice the wife of Thomas Cartwrite defendt a Jury of women…being Impaneled did in open Court upon their oaths declare that they having delegently Searched the body of the sd Alice & cann find noe Suspitious marks whereby they can Judge her to be a witch butt onely what may and Is usuall on women.

Through lack of any further evidence, county justices stated:

> It is therefore the Judgment of the Court and ordered that shee bee acquitted and her husbands bond given for her appearance to bee given up.

1694—PHYLLIS MONEY

In 1694, William Earle of Westmoreland County accused Phyllis Money of casting spells and teaching witchcraft. On November 1, he claimed before the county court that Phyllis had put a spell over a horse owned by her own son-in-law, Henry Dunkin. Earle also added that Phyllis had instructed John Dunkin in how to be a wizard and her daughter on how to be a witch. The accusations were unproven, and the case was dismissed. Phyllis then countersued for damages but received nothing.

1695—ELIZABETH DUNKIN

Very possibly related to the earlier case of Phyllis Money in Westmoreland County, just the year before, Elizabeth Dunkin was accused by Henry Dunkin of being regularly suckled by the devil. The charges were not proven, and Elizabeth sued for forty thousand pounds of tobacco as damages against her reputation. The county justices awarded only forty pounds.

Considering the parties involved in both the 1694 and 1695 Westmoreland suits and countersuits, there appears to have been quite a bit of discord between members of the Dunkin family.

1695—ELEANOR MORRIS AND NELL CANE

In 1695, Anne Ball appears to have been beset by witches. She was sure that Eleanor Morris of King and Queen County was a witch and accused her of being a sorceress. Anne told all who would listen that Mrs. Morris had bewitched her and "had rid her severall days & nights almost to death." She "despaired" for her life and said that she could prove the accusations. She also claimed to have been visited and ridden twice by another woman of the county, Nell Cane.

Perplexed and angry, Eleanor's husband, William Morris, sued Mrs. Ball in the Essex County Court for slander. In the complaint, William stated that his wife had resided in King and Queen County (previously part of New Kent County) for thirty years, where she had both a good name and reputation. He went on to say that his wife "never was guilty of any conjuration, witchcraft or enchantment, charmes, or sorcery, or any other such act or acts whereby to hurt anybody." According to Morris, Mrs. Ball had acted with "an evil intent and malitious designe to deprive & destroy" Eleanor's reputation.

Twelve bystanders were sworn in as jury members to hear the complaint of slander. Mrs. Ball declared that she was not guilty of any defamation of character; however, she evidently could not prove her public statements, as she had so freely professed earlier.

The case was dismissed and a countersuit of slander started. The jury must have felt that Mrs. Ball was a "gossipmonger," because they found in favor of Eleanor Morris and assessed five hundred pounds of tobacco as damages for the plaintiff.

1698—JOHN AND ANNE BYRD

In 1698, Charles Kinsey and John Potts of Princess Anne County believed that Anne Byrd and her husband, John, had bewitched them. Kinsey claimed that Anne had ridden him from his house to a neighbor's, while Potts claimed she had ridden him along the seashore to his own house.

On July 8, the Byrds brought two separate suits against Kinsey and Potts for "falsely and scandalously" defaming their name and asking for damages of one hundred pounds sterling from each of them. The Byrds claimed that by Kinsey's and Potts's loose talk, the duo had "reported & rendered as if they were witches, or in league with the Devill."

The two defendants admitted their accusations. Potts stated that he "acknowledgeth that to his thoughts, apprehensions or best knowledge they did serve him Soe," while Kinsey declared that he might have dreamed the whole thing. The jury, after hearing the evidence, seemed to have had either reservations about the Byrds or sympathy for Kinsey and Potts. They found for the defendants in both suits.

1697/8, 1698, 1705/6, 1706
GRACE SHERWOOD

Toward the end of the seventeenth century, a woman named Grace Sherwood lived in Princess Anne County (Lower Norfolk County before 1691). She was destined to become the subject of the most involved and well-known witchcraft investigation to occur in colonial Virginia. Her name has survived well into the present day, as does her reputation as the "Virginia Witch."

Grace was born around 1660 and was the daughter of a carpenter, John White. By 1680, it is known she was married to James Sherwood, a planter. The Sherwoods had at least three sons and resided in Lynnhaven Parish. Apparently neither James or Grace could read or write, as they signed their names with an X.

Grace's troubles started in 1697 when Richard Capps began speaking of her as witch. No formal accusation was made to the county court, but Capps's talk upset the Sherwoods to the extent that they felt the need to take legal action.

On February 4, 1697/8, James and Grace brought suit for defamation against Capps to the sum of fifty pounds sterling. Richard Capps did not appear in court that day to answer the charge, and the suit was continued to the next court session. It is not known exactly what happened between Capps and the Sherwoods, but sometime before the scheduled court day, the two parties apparently worked the matter out between them, as the suit was dismissed by the agreement of all concerned one month later, on March 3.

Within six months after she settled the matter against Richard Capps, Grace once again found her neighbors speaking of her as a witch. Now John Gisburne, a constable of the county, and his wife, Jane, were spreading the story that Grace had "bewitched their pigs to Death and bewitched their Cotton." At the same time, another woman, Elizabeth Barnes, made an extraordinary declaration. She claimed that Mrs. Sherwood "came to her one night," apparently without waking her husband, Anthony Barnes, who was sleeping beside her, "and rid her and went out the key hole or crack of the door like a black Catt."

To counter these accusations, Grace and her husband, James, brought separate lawsuits for slander against John and Jane Gisburne and Anthony and Elizabeth Barnes on September 10, 1698. The suits claimed that the defendants had "defamed and abused the said Grace in her good name and reputation," and asked for one hundred pounds sterling from each of the couples. As added weight to their argument, Grace's husband, James, brought nine witnesses to the court session to testify against the statements made by John Gisburne and Elizabeth Barnes. Present to serve as witnesses for Grace were Susanna Williams, John Lewis and his wife, Thomas Williams and his wife, Owen Macgrary, Edward Baker and John James.

A jury of twelve freeholders was formed from the court's bystanders, and both cases were heard. Both Constable Gisburne and Mrs. Barnes pleaded not guilty. The witnesses against them were heard, there was a short deliberation and in each case the jury foreman brought in a simple decision: "Wee of the jury find for the Defendant."

It was not a good day for the Sherwoods. In addition to having lost both suits and receiving nothing in damages, James Sherwood was required to pay the court costs involved in the transportation and attendance of his nine witnesses for four days of court.

James Sherwood died in 1701, leaving no will. Upon a request by Grace to the court to allow her to administer the estate, the Princess Anne County Court instructed the sheriff to summon two appraisers to appear at her house and inventory James's estate and its value. The appraisers, Edward Cannon and Richard Bonney, seemed to have done a thorough job. Among other things, they listed bedding, furniture, chests, household goods, cider casks, tools, an old gun and "one old poore mangy Scabby horse." Rounding out the inventory were six ewes and a ram. They estimated the total of the estate to be worth three thousand pounds of tobacco. Grace also informed the court that she possessed some saddles, five head of cattle and seven hogs, but the court does not seem to have amended the estate account.

Between James's death and late 1705, Grace lived with the continuing animosity of her of her neighbors. Evidently, previous lawsuits against those who had slandered her as a witch did little to deter the rumors and gossip.

In late November or early December 1705, Grace seems to have gotten into a brawl with Elizabeth Hill, a neighbor who had called her a witch, and immediately went to court charging assault and battery. The particulars of the fight are not known, but on December 7, 1705, Grace sued Luke Hill and his wife, Elizabeth, "in an action of Trespass of assault and battery, setting forth how the defendant's wife had assaulted, bruised, maimed and barbarously beaten the plaintiff." Grace asked for fifty pounds sterling in damages.

Through their attorney, Richard Corbitt, the Hills pleaded not guilty. A jury of freeholders was impaneled and sworn to hear the case. After a short deliberation, the jury found in Grace Sherwood's favor but awarded her only twenty shillings, or one pound, as damages.

Although the judgment represented only one-fiftieth of what Grace asked, Luke Hill and his wife decided that they needed complete vindication. Whether they were reacting in anger or they truly believed that Grace was a witch and a threat to the community, they went forward to prove their accusations and formally instituted a charge of witchcraft against her.

On January 3, 1705/6, the matter came before the justices of Princess Anne County. The complaint stated that Grace had bewitched Elizabeth Hill and petitioned that the justices investigate the "suspicion of witchcraft." Unfortunately, there was not much to investigate, as Grace failed to appear in court to answer the charge. The sheriff was ordered to have Grace present at the next court session.

On February 6 and 7, the court met again, with Grace in attendance. The justices seemingly wished to end the matter and ordered Luke Hill to pay all the fees involved in the complaint if he continued. Hill persisted, and the justices instructed the sheriff to summon a jury of women for the purpose of searching Grace's person for suspicious marks, indicating a pact with the devil. The case was continued until the next month.

The court next came together on March 7, with nine justices present. The summoned jury of women was sworn and proceeded to "make due inquiry and inspection into all circumstances." As in other cases, this meant that Grace was probably taken into a private room or home where she was stripped and her body searched for incriminating marks. If the justices were truly attempting to end the matter, they received a

Examination of a Witch, by T.H. Matteson, 1853. *Public domain.*

surprise when the jury delivered their findings: "Wee of the jury have Serchtt Grace Sherwood and found Two things like titts wth Severall other Spotts."

It is interesting to note that the same Elizabeth Barnes who had several years before been involved in a slander suit instigated by Grace served as the forewoman of the jury.

The justices of Princess Anne County now faced a quandary. They possibly had a real witch on their hands and were unsure of exactly how to proceed. Luke Hill and his complaint were referred to the governor's council and queen's attorney in Williamsburg:

> *At a council held at Her Majesties Royall Capitol 28th day of March 1706: Luke Hill by his petition informing the Board that one Grace Sherwood of Princess Anne County being suspected of witchcraft upon his complaint to that county court that she bewitched the petitioners wife, the court ordered a jury of women to search the said Grace Sherwood, who upon search brought in a verdict against the said Grace, but the court not knowing how to proceed to judgment thereon, the petitioner prays that the attorney General may be directed to prosecute the said Grace for the same.*

The governor's council ordered that the queen's attorney, Stephens Thompson, consider the matter and make a report back the following month. Accordingly, on April 16, Mr. Thompson delivered his opinion:

> *Upon perusal of the above order of this honorable Board I do conceive and am of the opinion that the charge or accusation is too general that the county court ought to make further examination of the matters of fact and to have proceeded therein pursuant to the directions and powers of County Courts given by the late act of Assembly in criminal cases made and provided and if they thought there was sufficient cause to (according to law) committed her to the General prison of this Colony whereby it would have come regularly before the General Court and whereupon I should have prepared a bill for the Grand jury and if thy found it I should have prosecuted it.*
>
> *I therefore with humble submission offer and conceive it proper that the said County Court do make further enquiry into the matter, and if they are of opinion there be cause they act according to the above law and I shall be ready to present a Bill and if found proceed thereon.*

Upon receipt of the queen's attorney's opinion, the justices of Princess Anne County decided to take his advice and continue their examination. Because they felt a "great Cause of Suspicion," they immediately ordered that the sheriff take Grace into custody until she could give a bond for her appearance at the next session of the court. Following the advice of Dalton's *Country Justice* concerning puppets and images, they also instructed the county sheriff and local constable to make a search of "the Sd Graces House and all Suspicious places Carefully for all Images and Such like things as may in any way Strengthen the Suspicion."

On June 6 and 7, 1706, Grace stood before the justices of the county and the investigation continued as a criminal suit. The deputy queen's attorney of the county, Maximillian Boush, brought several witnesses forward. In due course, they were each sworn and gave evidence against Grace. She offered no excuses and had little to say in her own defense. At this point, it was discovered that although the sheriff had summoned another jury of women to come forward to search Grace a second time, not one had shown up at the court. Therefore, the sheriff was ordered to summon them to appear a second time, not to search Grace, but "To be Dealt with according to the uttmost Severity of the Law," because of their contempt. The sheriff was told to summon a third jury to search Grace's person and to have everyone at the next session of the court.

On Friday, July 5, the court convened once again. Unfortunately for the justices, the sheriff could not gather another jury of women together. Doubtful that they would be able to assemble twelve women to carry out an examination, the court decided on another test. Stating that they were "willing to have all means possible tryed either to acquit her or to Give more Strength to the Suspician that She might be Dealt with as Deserved," the justices ordered the sheriff to try her by ducking or swimming. This ancient test would determine her guilt or innocence by placing her in a body of water to see if she would float.

The justices expressed at least a small bit of concern over Grace's well-being. The test was postponed because of "the weather being very Rainy and Bad" and they did not wish to "endanger her health."

Five days later, at ten o'clock in the morning of Wednesday, July 10, Grace was taken to a pond on the plantation of John Harper. There, she was stripped to her shift and inspected by several women to ensure that she was concealing nothing that would affect the test. She was then bound, hand to foot, with a rope around her body. With the help of men in a boat, whose purpose was to "preserve her from Drowning," the sheriff lowered Grace

Virginia Department of Historic Resources
Marker for Grace Sherwood. *Courtesy of
Bob Ruegsegger.*

into the pond from a point of land that survives to the present day as "Witchduck Point." The court and bystanders watched carefully to observe whether she floated (guilty) or sank beneath the water's surface (innocent).

Before the assembled gathering, Grace failed the test. She stayed afloat "Contrary to Custom." Being brought ashore, and presumably still wet, Grace was once again searched by five "ancient women," whom the sheriff had managed to gather. After their examination, they declared:

> [O]n Oath that She is not like them nor noe Other woman that they knew of, having two Things like titts on her private parts of a Black Coller being Blacker than the Rest of her Body.

By now the justices were quite ready to pass the whole matter on to the queen's attorney in Williamsburg. The court ordered the sheriff to

> take the Sd Grace Into his Custody and to Commit her body to the Common Gaol of this County there to Secure her by irons, or Otherwise there to Remaine till Such time as he Shall be otherwise Directed in ordr for her coming to the Common Gaole of the country to bee brought to a Future Tryall there.

Here the exact disposition of Grace Sherwood's case falls into dispute, and one can only speculate on what actually followed, as the surviving records are silent. Grace could have spent time in the county jail and been released. She may have been whipped or otherwise punished and then released. She may have been, as ordered, sent to the General Court and examined in Williamsburg. There, the governor's council may have found her innocent and released her. On the other hand, the officials may have found her guilty and imprisoned or punished her by some means. Unfortunately, the legal records of the General Court of colonial Virginia were largely destroyed during the Civil War.

Statue of Grace Sherwood in Virginia Beach. *Courtesy of Bob Ruegsegger.*

IN MEMORY OF
GRACE WHITE SHERWOOD
1660 — 1740
HEALER OF SICK WITH HERBS
CONVICTED AS A WITCH
SHE SURVIVED VIRGINIA'S ONLY
TRIAL BY DUCKING IN THE
LYNNHAVEN RIVER
JULY 10, 1706
NAME CLEARED ... GOVERNOR

Above: Street sign at intersection of Sherwood Lane and Witchduck Road in Virginia Beach. *Courtesy of Bob Ruegsegger.*

Right: Memorial stone to Grace Sherwood in Virginia Beach. *Courtesy of Bob Ruegsegger.*

Whatever actually happened to her after her imprisonment by the Princess Anne County authorities, she survived. The extant records indicate that Grace survived to be an old woman.

In June 1714, she received a grant for 145 acres of land that had belonged to her father from Lieutenant Governor Alexander Spotswood. Unlike her husband, she wrote out a will in later life, dated 1733. It was probated in October 1740, leaving her property to her three sons. Thus, the "Virginia Witch" lived for thirty-four years after her examination.

In 1973, Louisa Venable Kyle published a children's book, *The Witch of Pungo and Other Historical Stories of the Early Colonies*. It popularized and resurrected Grace Sherwood's name to many of the local community who had never heard of her. By the beginning of the twenty-first century, Grace's story had acquired quite a bit of legend and witchcraft lore. There are many stories, such as she was a beautiful woman that others were jealous of, that she was an herbalist and healer and that she was an early advocate of women's rights. None of this can be documented in any period record. Nevertheless, she has become a local folk hero, and in 2006 the governor of Virginia was persuaded to issue her a state pardon, which is perplexing, since there is no existing record of Grace ever being convicted of anything.

TODAY, A VISITOR TO Virginia Beach will find a Sherwood Lane and a Witchduck Road along with a bronze statue of Grace Sherwood near a local hospital and a memorial marker near a local church.

Such is the power of witchcraft even today.

1706—ALICE CORNICK

While Grace Sherwood was undergoing her examination as a witch by the justices of Princess Anne County, Alice Cornick was involved as a witness in a slander suit before the same court. Unfortunately for all concerned in the case, the dispute was between Thomas Ivy, Alice's son from a first marriage, and Joel Cornick, her stepson from a second. Sometime during, or immediately after the proceedings, a neighbor, Thomas Phillips, publicly referred to Alice as "a witch." It is quite possible that his comments were influenced by the recent local events surrounding Grace Sherwood.

Because of his remarks, Thomas Ivy made a formal complaint on behalf of his mother against Phillips during the July session of the court. With the county justices already distracted over the matter of Grace Sherwood, they must have been quite relieved when Phillips appeared at the September session and admitted that he had wrongfully libeled Alice as a witch. He publicly apologized, and the justices ordered Phillips to pay the court costs of the suit.

1706—MARY ROOKES (NORTH CAROLINA)

During the summer of 1706, as the legal proceedings involving Grace Sherwood and Alice Cornick were progressing separately in Princess Anne County, it is curious to note that less than fifty miles south, in North Carolina, another woman was being defamed by her neighbors as a witch.

In July 1706, Mary Rookes of the Perquimans District of Albemarle brought suit in the North Carolina General Court against Thomas Collings and Walter Tanner. Apparently, the two men had made several accusations of witchcraft against Mary. Collings had stated that she was "a Dammed Witch and have bewitched my wife." Tanner also claimed to have been bewitched and indicated that he could prove it. Mary petitioned the court that their talk had damaged her "Good name, Fame, Credit, and reputation." She asked for one hundred pounds sterling from each of the defendants as damages. A separate jury was sworn in each suit, and Mary was awarded a total of six shillings.

Perhaps the accusations against Mary Rookes were prompted by the court cases and gossip occurring in nearby Princess Anne County. In 1706, North Carolina was thinly populated, and much of Albemarle County's contact with the world was through southeastern Virginia. The court records indicate that like Grace Sherwood, Mary had long been thought to be a witch, having brought suit against another neighbor in 1701, who claimed that she had "Haggridden him."

1730—MARY (SERVANT OF JOHN SAMFORD)

Possibly the last case of witchcraft seen by a Virginia court occurred in October 1730 in Richmond County. A white indentured servant, known only as Mary, belonging to John Samford, was committed to the county jail on the charge of using "Inchantment, Charm, witchcraft, or Conjuration, to tell where Treasure is, or where goods left may be found." It is quite possible that the unfortunate Mary was merely telling fortunes. On court day, Mary was examined by the county magistrates and heard several persons speak against her. Apparently, the evidence was sufficient, for the justices ruled that:

> It is the opinion of this Court that the said Mary is Guilty of what is laid to her Charge, it is therefore ordered that the Sheriff take her and Carry her to the Common Whipping post, and give her thirty-nine lashes on her bare back well laid on.

It is worthy of mention that under the Witchcraft Statute of James I, Mary's crime was considered "petit" witchcraft, punishable by a year in jail and publicly confessing her sins. The Richmond County court seemingly decided to end the matter at once, showing how Virginia justices altered existing law to their community's needs.

EPILOGUE

Although the court records are far from complete, there seems to be no serious mention of witchcraft before a Virginia court after 1730. The Age of Enlightenment seemed to be displacing earlier beliefs. With the repeal of the witchcraft statutes in 1736, Virginians seemed to have been vindicated in the restraint exercised by their courts. The passing of a new law, however, did not mean that the idea of witchcraft had suddenly ceased to exist.

On the first page of the January 20, 1738 edition of the *Virginia Gazette*, the following letter and story were reprinted from an English newspaper:

> *London, July 21, 1737*
> *Sir,*
> *I send you enclos'd a very remarkable Letter concerning the late cruel Usage of a poor old Woman in Bedfordshire, who was suspected of being a Witch. You will see by it, that the late Law for Abolishing the Act against Witches has not abolish'd the Credulity of the Country People; but I hope it has made proper Provision for punishing their Barbarity on such Occasions.*
> *I am Sir*
> *Yours, &c. A B.*

Extract of a Letter about the Tryal of a Witch.

SIR,

The People here are so predjudic'd in the Belief of Witches that you would think yourself in Lapland, was you to hear their ridiculous Stories. There is not a Village in the Neighborhood but has Two or Three. About a Week ago I was present at the Ceremony of Ducking a Witch; a particular Account of which, may not perhaps be disagreeable to you.

An Old Woman of about 60 Years of Age had long lain under an Imputation of Witchcraft; who, being willing (for her own Sake and her Children's) to clear herself, consented to be duck'd; and the Parish Officers promis'd her a Guinea, if she should sink; The Place appointed for the Operation, was in the River Oust, by a Mill; there were, I believe, 500 Spectators; About 11 o'Clock in the Forenoon, the Woman came, and was tied up in a wet Sheet, all but her Face and Hands; her Toes were tied close together, as were also her Thumbs, and her Hands tied to the small of her Legs; They fasten'd a Rope about her Middle, and then pull'd off her Cap to search for Pins, for their Notion is, if they have but one Pin about 'em, they won't sink.

When all Preliminaries were settled, she was thrown in; but, unhappily for the poor Creature,s he floated, tho' her Head was all the while under Water; Upon this there was a confus'd Cry, A Witch! A Witch! Hang her! Drown her! She was in the Water about one Minute and a Half, and was then taken out half drown'd; when she had recovered Breath, the Experiment was repeated twice more, but with the same Success, for she floated each Time; which was a plain Demonstration of Guilt to the ignorant Multitude; For notwithstanding the poor Creature was laid upon the Grass, speechless, and almost dead, they were so far from shewing her any Pity or Compassion, that they strove who should be the most forward in loading her with Reproaches, Such is the dire Effect of popular Predjudice! As for my Part, I stood against the Torrent, and when I had cut the Strings which tied her, had her carried back to the Mill, and endeavored to convince the People of the Uncertainty of the Experiment, and offer'd to lay Five to One, that any Woman of her Age, so tied up in a loose Sheet, would float, but all to no Purpose, for I was very near being mobb'd. Some Time after, the Woman came out; and one of the Company happen'd to mention another Experiment to try a Witch, which was to weigh her against the Church Bible; for a Witch it seems, could not outweigh it. I immediately seconded that Motion (as thinking it might be of Service to the poor Woman) and

Primitive early English woodcut of a witch being ducked. *Public domain.*

made use of an Argument, which (tho' as weak as King Jame's for their not sinking) had some Weight with the People; for I told them, if she was a Witch, she certainly dealt with the Devil; and as the Bible was undoubtedly the Word of God, it must weigh more than all the Works of the Devil. This seem'd reasonable to several; and those that did not think it so, could not answer it; At last, the Question was carried, and she was weighed against the Bible; which weighing about twelve Pounds, she outweighed it. This convinc'd some, and stagger'd others; but some who believ'd thro' thick and thin, went away fully assured, that she was a Witch, and endeavored to inculcate that Belief into all others.

Hopefully, by this time, most Virginians would shake their heads in amazement at such nonsense.

NOTES ON SOURCES
AND DOCUMENTS OF
COLONIAL VIRGINIA

In order to learn about the cases of witchcraft that appeared in Virginia courts, it is not only necessary to review the scant number of secondary sources available but also examine the existing original documents and court records of the period.

During the seventeenth and early eighteenth centuries, Virginia's court records, whether for a specific county or for the General Court, were generally maintained by the clerk of that court. Some clerks were diligent and maintained fine records, safeguarding them over the years. Some were less conscientious, keeping their records at their own homes in trunks or boxes that were left to mold and mildew as they grew older and less likely to be needed. As Virginia grew, larger counties were divided into smaller ones. The American Revolution and especially the Civil War disrupted courts, and records were moved, hidden, misplaced or lost to fire or vandalism. By the late nineteenth century, when historic preservation became important to many Virginians, there were large gaps in the surviving records.

In attempting to examine and transcribe the remaining court documents, one is faced with the challenge of deciphering the handwriting, spelling and varieties of abbreviations of numerous clerks over the years.

Court records of the colonial period were not the verbatim documents prepared by court recorders and stenographers of today. Generally, clerks would make notes that would later (sometimes, much later) be entered, possibly with additional information or margin notes, into bound record books. These became the official court records.

Depending on the clerk, you may find excellent and easy-to-read handwriting or a barely discernable scrawl that can be extremely frustrating. Many court clerks practiced their own versions of shorthand and abbreviations, in which they attempted to condense lengthy legal documents and save time.

Adding to this frustration, clerks commonly spelled many words and names as they sounded. This could lead to several spellings (or misspellings) of the same person's name, sometimes within the same document. During research, this can cloud the issue of exactly who is involved in a case.

Finally, even the exact dates of certain records can be difficult to determine. Before 1752, England and its North American colonies used the Gregorian calendar. Besides being several days behind much of the rest of the world (eleven days in 1752), the first day of the year was not January 1 but March 25, the Feast of the Annunciation. Therefore, a typical year would run from March 25 to the following March 24. What might be 1696 in England and Virginia was 1697 in Germany or France.

In an attempt to coexist with the rest of the world, English dates were written using both the "old style" and "new style." For example, from January 1 until March 24, a date would be written 1696/7, meaning the event occurred in the civil year (March 25–March 24) of 1696 but in the calendar year (January 1–December 31) of 1697.

It was confusing even then.

Appendix A

THE WITCHCRAFT ACTS

The following are basic transcripts of the English Witchcraft Acts of 1542, 1562, 1604 and 1736.

THE WITCHCRAFT ACT OF 1542 (HENRY VIII)

Bill ayest conjuraracons & wichecraftes and sorcery and enchantmants.

Where dyvers and sundrie persones unlawfully have devised and practised Invocacons and conjuracons of Sprites, ptending by such meanes to understande and get Knowlege for their owne lucre in what place treasure of golde and Silver shulde or mought be founde or had in the earthe or other secrete places, and also have used and occupied wichecraftes inchauntement and sorceries to the distruccon of their neighbours persones and goodes, And for execucon of their saide false devyses and practises have made or caused to be made dyvers Images and pictures of men women childrene Angelles or develles beastes or fowles, and also have made Crownes Septures Swordes rynges glasses and other things, and other things, and gyving faithe & credit to suche fantasticall practises have dygged up and pulled downe an infinite nombre of Crosses within this Realme, and taken upon them to declare and tell where things lost or stollen shulde be become; whiche things cannot be used and exercised but to the great offence of Godes lawe, hurt and damage of the Kinges Subjectes, and losse of the sowles of suche Offenders, to the greate dishonor of God, Infamy and disquyetnes of the Realme:

For Reformacon wherof be it enacted by the Kyng oure Soveraigne Lorde with thassent of the Lordes spuall and temporall and the Comons in this present Parliament assembled and by auctoritie of the same, that yf any persone or persones. after the first daye of Maye next comyng, use devise practise or exercise, or cause to be used devysed practised or exercised, any Invocacons or conjuracons of Sprites wichecraftes enchauntmentes or sorceries, to thentent to get or fynde money or treasure,or to waste consume or destroy any persone in his bodie membres or goodes, or to pvoke any persone to unlawfull love, or for any other unlawfull intente or purpose, or by occacon or color of suche thinges or any of them. or for dispite of Cryste, or for lucre of money, dygge up or pull downe any Crosse or Crosses, or by suche Invocacons or conjuracons of Sprites wichecraftes enchauntementes or sorcerie or any of them take upon them to tell or declare where goodes stollen or lost shall become, That then all and every suche Offence and Offences, frome the saide first day of May next comyng shalbe demyde accepted and adjuged Felonye; And that all and every persone and persones offendyng as is abovesaide their Councellors Abettors and Procurors and every of them from the saide first day of Maye shallbe demyde accepted and adjuged a Felon and Felones; And thoffender and offenders contrarie to this Acte. being therof lawfullie convicte before suche as shall have power and auctoritie to here and determyn felonyes, shall have and suffre such paynes of deathe losse and forfaytures of their lands tentes goodes and Catalles as in cases of felonie by the course of the Comon lawes of this Realme, And also shall lose p'vilege of Clergie and Sayntuarie.

The Witchcraft Act of 1562 (Elizabeth I)

An Act agaynst Conjuracons Inchantments and Witchecraftes.

Where at this present, there ys no ordinarye ne condigne Punishement provided agaynst the Practisers of the wicked Offences of Conjuracons and Invocacons of evill Spirites, and of Sorceries Enchauntmentes Charmes and Witchecraftes, the wch Offences by force of a Statute made in the xxxiij yere of the Reigne of the late King Henry the Eyghthe were made to bee Felonye, and so continued untill the sayd Statute was repealed by Thacte and Statute of Repeale made in the first yere of the Reigne of the late King Edwarde the vjth; sythens the Repeale wherof many fantasticall and devilishe psons have devised and practised Invocacons and Conjuracons of evill and wicked Spirites, and alwe used and practised Wytchecraftes Enchantementes Charms and Sorceries, to the Destruccoon of the Psons and Goodes of their Neighebours and other Subjectes of this Realme, and for other lewde Intentes and Purposes contrarye to the Lawes of Almighty God, to the Perill of theyr owne Soules, and to the great Infamye and Disquietnes of this Realme:

For REFORMACON wherof bee it enacted by the Quenes Matie with thassent of the Lordes Spuall and Temporall and the Comons in this pnte Pliament assembled, and by the aucthoritee of the same, That yf any pson or psons after the first daye of June nexte coming, use practise or exercise any Invocacons or Conjuracons of evill and wicked Spirites, to or for any Intent or Purpose; or els if any pson or psons after the said first daye of June shall use practise or exercise any Wytchecrafte Enchantment Charme or Sorcerie, wherby any pson shall happen to bee killed or destroyed, that then aswell every suche offendor or offendors in Invocacons and Conjuracons as ys aforesayd, their Concellors & Aidours, as also every suche offendor or offendors in Witchecrafte Enchantement Charme or Sorcerie whereby the Deathe of anny pson dothe ensue, their Aidours and Concellors, being of either of the said Offences laufully convicted and attainted, shall suffer paynes of Deathe as a Felon or Felons, and shall lose the Priviledg and Benefite of Sanctuarie & Clergie: Saving to the Wief of such persone her Title of Dower, and also to the Heyre and Successour of suche pson his or theyr Tytles of Inheritaunce Succession and other Rightes, as thoughe nu suche Attayndour of the Auncestour or Predecessour had been hadd or made.

And further bee yt enacted by thaucthoritee aforesayd, That if any pson or psons, after the saide forst daye of June nexte comyng, shall use practise or exercyse any Wytchecrafte Enchauntement Charme or Sorcerie, wherby any pon shall happen to bee wasted consumed or lamed in his or her Bodye or Member, or wherby any Goodes or Cattles of any pson shal bee destroyed wasted or impayred, then every suche offendour or Offendours their Councelloures and Aydoures, being therof laufully caonvicted, shall for his or their first Offence or Offences, suffer Imprisonment by the Space of one whole Yere, without Bayle or Mayneprise, and once in every

Quarter of the said Yere, shall in some Market towne, upon the Market Daye or at such tyme as any Fayer shalbee kepte there, stande openly upon the Pillorie by the Space of Syxe Houres, and there shall openly confesse his or her Erroure and Offence; and for the Seconde offence, being as ys aforesayd laufully convicted or attaynted shall suffer deathe as a Felon, and shall lose the Privilege of Clergie and Sanctuarye: Saving to the Wief [as above]

Provided alwaies, That yf the Offendour, in any of the Cases aforesayd for whiche the paynes of Deathe shall ensue, shall happen to bee a Peere of this Realme, then his Triall thereyn to be hadd by hys Peeres, as yt ys used in cases of Felonye or Treason and not otherwyse.

And further to thintent that all maner of practise use or exercise of Witchecrafte Enchantement Charme or Sorcerye shoulde bee from hensforthe utterly avoyded abolished and taken away; Bee it enacted by thaucthoritee of this pnte Pliament. That yf any pson or psons shall from and after the sayd first daye of June nexte coming, take upon him or them, by Witchecrafte Enchantement Charme or Sorcerie, to tell or declare in what Place any Treasure of Golde or Sylver shoulde or might bee founde or had in the Earthe or other secret Places, or where Goodes or Thinges lost or stollen should bee founde or becume, or shall use or practise anye Sorcerye Enchantement Charme or Witchcrafte, to thintent to provoke any pson to unlaufull love, or to hurte or destroye any pson in his or her Body, Member or Goodes; that then every suche pson or psons so offending, and being therof laufully convicted, shall for the said offence suffer Imprysonement by the space of One whole yere without Bayle or Mayneprise, and once in every Quarter of the said Yere, shall in some Market towne, upon the Marcket Daye or at such tyme as any Fayer shalbee kepte there, stande openly upon the Pillorie by the Space of Syxe Houres, and there shall openly confesse his or her Erroure and Offence; And yf anye pson or psons, beyng once convicted of the same Offences as ys aforesayd, doo eftesones ppetrate and comitt the lyke Offence, that then every suche Offendour beyng therof the seconde tyme convicted as ys aforesaid, shall forfaitee unto the Quenes Majestie her heires and successoures, all his Goodes and Cattelles and suffer Imprysonement during Lyef.

THE WITCHCRAFT ACT OF 1604
(JAMES I)

The Witchcraft Statute of King James I was passed in June 1604 and dramatically changed the law regarding witchcraft in Great Britain and Virginia.

An Acte against conjuration Witchcrafte and dealinge with evill and wicked Spirits.

BE it enacted by the King our Sovraigne Lorde the Lordes Spirituall and Temporall and the Comons in this p'sent Parliament assembled, and by the authoritie of the same, That the Statute made in the fifth yeere of the Raigne of our late Sov'aigne Ladie of the most famous and happy memorie Queene Elizabeth, intituled An Acte againste Conjurations Inchantments and witchcraftes, be from the Feaste of St. Michaell the Archangell nexte cominge, for and concerninge all Offences to be committed after the same Feaste, utterlie repealed.

AND for the better restrayning of saide Offenses, and more severe punishinge the same, be it further enacted by the authoritie aforesaide, That if any pson or persons after the saide Feaste of Saint Michaell the Archangell next comeing, shall use practise or exercsise any Invocation or Conjuration of any evill and spirit, or shall consult covenant with entertaine employ feede or rewarde any evill and wicked Spirit to or for any intent or purpose; or take any dead man woman or child out of his her or theire grave or any other place where the dead body resteth, or the skin, bone or any other parte of any dead person, to be imployed or used in any manner of Witchecrafte, Sorcerie, Charme or Inchantment; or shall use practise or exercise any Witchcrafte Sorcerie, Charme or Incantment wherebie any pson shall be killed destroyed wasted consumed pined or lamed in his or her bodie, or any parte therof; then that everie such Offendor or Offendors theire Ayders Abettors and Counsellors, being of the saide Offences dulie and lawfullie convicted and attainted, shall suffer pains of deathe as a Felon or Felons, and shall loose the priviledge and benefit of Cleargie and Sanctuarie.

AND FURTHER, to the intent that all manner of practise use or exercise of declaring by Witchcrafte, Inchantment Charme or Sorcerie should be from henceforth utterlie avoyded abolished and taken away, Be it enacted by the authorite of this p'sent Parliament, that if any pson or psons shall from and after the saide Feaste of Saint Michaell the Archangell next cominge, take upon him or them by Witchcrafte Inchantment Charme or Sorcerie to tell or declare in what place any treasure of Golde or silver should or had in the earth or other secret places, or where Goodes or Thinges loste or stollen should be founde or become; or to the intent to Pvoke any person to unlawfull love, or wherebie any Cattell or Goods of any pson shall be destroyed wasted or impaired, or to hurte or destroy any Pson in his bodie, although the same be not effected and done: that then all and everie such pson or psons so offendinge, and beinge therof lawfullie convicted, shall for the said Offence suffer Imprisonment by the space of one whole yeere, without baile or maineprise, and once in everie quarter of the saide yeere, shall in some Markett Towne, upon the Markett Day, or at such tyme as any Faire shalbe kept there, stande openlie upon the Pillorie by the space of sixe houres, and there shall openlie confesse his or her error and offence ; And if any pson or psons beinge once convicted of the same offences as is aforesaide, doe eftsones ppetrate and comit the like offence, that then everie such Offender, beinge of the saide offences the second tyme lawfullie and duelie convicted and attainted as is aforesaide, shall suffer paines of deathe as a Felon or Felons, and shall loose the benefitt and priviledge of Clergie and Sanctuarie: Saving to the wife of such person as shall offend in any thinge contrarie to this Acte ; her title of dower; and also to the heire and successor of everie such person his or theire titles of Inheritance Succession and other Rights, as though no such Attaindor or the Ancestor or Predecessor had been made; Provided alwaies that if the offender in any cases aforesaide shall happen to be a Peere of this Realme, then his Triall therein is to be had by his Peeres, as it is used in cases of Felonie or Treason and not otherwise.

The Witchcraft Act of 1736 (George II)

An Act to repeal the Statute made in the First Year of the Reign of King James the First, intituled, An Act against Conjuration, Witchcraft, and dealing with evil and wicked Spirits, except so much thereof as repeals an Act of the Fifth Year of the Reign of Queen Elizabeth, Against Conjurations, Inchantments, and Witchcrafts, and to repeal an Act passed in the Parliament of Scotland in the Ninth Parliament of Queen Mary, intituled, Anentis Witchcrafts, and for punishing such Persons as pretend to exercise or use any kind of Witchcraft, Sorcery, Inchantment, or Conjuration.

Appendix A

Be it enacted by the King's most Excellent Majesty, by and with the Advice and Consent of the Lords Spiritual and Temporal, and Commons, in this present Parliament assembled, and by the Authority of the same, That the Statute made in the First Year of the Reign of King James the First, intituled, An Act against Conjuration, Witchcraft, and dealing with evil and wicked Spirits, shall, from the Twenty-fourth Day of June next, be repealed and utterly void, and of none effect (except so much thereof as repeals the Statute made in the Fifth Year of the Reign of Queen Elizabeth) intituled, An Act against Conjurations, Inchantments, and Witchcrafts.

And be it further enacted by the Authority aforesaid, That from and after the said Twenty-fourth Day of June, the Act passed in the Parliament of Scotland, in the Ninth Parliament of Queen Mary, intituled, Anentis Witchcrafts, shall be, and is hereby repealed.

And be it further enacted, That from and after the said Twenty-fourth Day of June, no Prosecution, Suit, or Proceeding, shall be commenced or carried on against any Person or Persons for Witchcraft, Sorcery, Inchantment, or Conjuration, or for charging another with any such Offence, in any Court whatsoever in Great Britain.

And for the more effectual preventing and punishing of any Pretences to such Arts or Powers as are before mentioned, whereby ignorant Persons are frequently deluded and defrauded; be it further enacted by the Authority aforesaid, That if any Person shall, from and after the said Twenty-fourth Day of June, pretend to exercise or use any kind of Witchcraft, Sorcery, Inchantment, or Conjuration, or undertake to tell Fortunes, or pretend, from his or her Skill or Knowledge in any occult or crafty Science, to discover where or in what manner any Goods or Chattels, supposed to have been stolen or lost, may be found, every Person, so offending, being thereof lawfully convicted on Indictment or Information in that part of Great Britain called England, or on Indictment or Libel in that part of Great Britain called Scotland, shall, for every such Offence, suffer Imprisonment by the Space of one whole Year without Bail or Mainprize, and once in every Quarter of the said Year, in some Market Town of the proper County, upon the Market Day, there stand openly on the Pillory by the Space of One Hour, and also shall (if the Court by which such Judgement shall be given shall think fit) be obliged to give Sureties for his or her good Behaviour, in such Sum, and for such Time, as the said Court shall judge proper according to the Circumstances of the Offence, and in such case shall be further imprisoned until such Sureties be given.

PREFACE TO *DAEMONOLOGIE*

Written by King James VI of Scotland (King James I of England) Originally printed in Edinburgh, 1597

THE PREFACE

to the Reader.

The fearefull aboundinge at this time in this countrie, of these detestable slaves of the Devill, the Witches or enchanters, hath moved me (beloved reader) to dispatch in post, this following treatise of mine, not in any way (as I protest) to serve for a shew of my learning and ingine, but onely (mooved of conscience) to preasse thereby, so farre as I can, to resolve the doubting harts of many; both that such assaultes of Sathan are most certainly practized, and that the instrumentes thereof, merits most severely to be punished: against the damnable opinions of two principally in our age, whereof the one called SCOT an Englishman, is not ashamed in publike print to deny, that ther can be such a thing as Witch-craft: and so mainteines the old error of the Sadducees, in denying of spirits. The other called WIERUS, a German Phisition, sets out a publick apologie for all these crafts-folks, wherby, procuring for their impunitie, he plainely bewrayes himselfe to have bene one of that profession. And for to make this treatise the more pleasant and facill, I have put it in forme of dialogue, which I have divided into three bookes: The first speaking of Magie in general, and Necromancie in special. The second of Sorcerie and Witch-craft: and the thirde, conteines a discourse of all these kindes of spirits, and Spectres that appeares and trobles persones: together with a conclusion of the whol work. My intention in this labour, is only to prove two things, as I have already said: the one, that such divelish artes have bene and are. The other, what exact triale and severe punishment they merite: and therefore reason , what kinde of things are possible to be performed in these arts, and by what naturall causes they may be, not that I touch every particular thing of the Devil's power, for that wer infinite: but onelie, to speak scholasticklie, (since this can not bee spoken in our language) I reason upon kind (genus) leaving appearance (species), and differences (differentia) to be comprehended therein. As for example, speaking of the power of Magiciens, in the first book and sixt Chapter: I say, that they can suddenly be brought unto them, al kindes of daintie disshes, by their familiar spirit: Since as a thiefe he delightes to steale and as a spirite, he can subtilie and suddenlie inough transport the same. Now under this kind (genus), may be comprehended al particulars, depending thereupon. Such as the bringing Wine out of the Wall, (as we have heard oft to have bene practised) and such others; which particulars, are sufficientlie proved by the reasons of the general. And such like in the second booke of Witch-craft in speciall, and fift Chap. I say and prove by diverse arguments, that Witches can, by the power of their Master, cur or cast on disseases: Now by these same reasones, that proves their power by the Devil of disseases in generall, is aswell proved their power in speciall: as of weakening the nature of some men, to make them unable for women: and making it to abound in others, more then the ordinary course of nature would permit. And such like in all other particular sicknesses; But one thing I wil pray thee to observe in all these places, where I reason upon the devils power, which is the different ends and scopes, that God as the first cause, and the Devill as his instrument and second cause shootes at in all these actiones of the Devil, (as Gods hang-man:) For where the devilles intention in them is ever to perish, either the soule or the body, or both of them, that he is so permitted to deale with: God by the contraries, drawes ever out of the eville glory to hmselfe, either by the wracke of the wicked in his justice, or by the tryall of the patient and amendment of the faithfull, being wakened up with that rod of correction. Having thus declared unto thee then, my full intention in this Treatise, thou wilt easelie excuse, I doubt not, as well my pretermitting, to declare the whole particular rites and secrets of these unlawfull artes: as also their infinite and wounderfull practices, as being neither of them pertinent to my purpose: the reason whereof, is given in the hinder ende of the first Chapter of the thirde booke: and who likes to be curious in these thinges, he may reade, if he will here of their practices, BODINUS Daemonomanie, collected with greater diligence, then written with judgement, together with their confessions, that have bene at this time apprehened. If he would know what hath bene the opinion of the Auncientes, concerning their power: he shall see it wel descrybed by HYPERIUS, and HEMMINGIUE, two late Germain writers: Besides innumerable other neoterick Theologues, that writes largelie upon that subject: And if he woulde knowe what are the particuler rites, and curiousities of these black arts (which is both unnecessaries and perilous,) he will finde it in the fourth book of CORNELIUS Agrippa, and in VIERUS, whomof I spak. And so wishing my pains in this Treatise (beloved Reader) to be effectual, in arming al them that reades the same, against thes above mentioned erroures, and recommending my good will to thy friendly acceptation, I bid thee hartely fare-well.

JAMES Rex.

Appendix C

A BRIEF CHRONOLOGY
OF WITCHCRAFT IN ENGLAND
AND SCOTLAND

Hanged witches from an English broadside, 1589. *Public domain.*

Belief in witchcraft in colonial Virginia did not exist in a vacuum. The following list is a brief timeline of what was occurring in England and Scotland in the sixteenth, seventeenth and eighteenth centuries. The listing is by no means complete, and only major witchcraft examinations are mentioned. Between 1590 and 1700, over 5 percent of all the cases heard in English county courts involved some mention of witchcraft. In the Home Circuit around London, the figure was as high as 13 percent. It is important to observe that many of the settlers arriving in Virginia throughout the seventeenth and early eighteenth centuries would have carried with them memories of these events.

1542

Witchcraft Act of 1542 (Henry VIII) is enacted. Witchcraft is a felony.

1547

Witchcraft Act of 1542 (Henry VIII) is repealed by Edward VI.

1563

Witchcraft Act of 1563 (Queen Elizabeth I) is enacted. Witchcraft is once again a felony, with conditions. Scottish Witchcraft Act of 1563 is also enacted.

1564

Elizabeth Lowys is the first person tried and convicted under the English Act of 1563.

1566

Witchcraft trials occur in Chelmsford. The first surviving pamphlet concerning English witchcraft, *The Examination and Confession of Cetaine Wytches*, is published.

1568

A large witch hunt occurs in Scotland, with about forty persons accused in Angus and the Mearns.

1579

Witchcraft trials occur at Windsor, Chelmsford and Abington.

1584

Reginald Scot publishes the *Discovery of Witchcraft*, disputing witchcraft.

1586

The English Statute of 1563 is legislated into Irish law.

1589

A series of storms prevents King James VI of Scotland from meeting his intended bride. Witchcraft is suspected. Witch trials occur in Chelmsford. King James VI becomes a firm believer in witchcraft.

1590

Trials of the "North Berwick witches" occur in Edinburgh. King James VI participates in the examinations.

1593

Witchcraft trials occur in Huntingdon.

1595

Witchcraft trials occur in Braynford and Barnett.

1596

Witchcraft trials occur in Edinburgh.

1597

King James VI publishes his treatise on witchcraft, *Daemonologie*. It is partially in a response to Reginald Scot's *Discovery of Witchcraft*.

1598

Witchcraft trials occur in Aberdeen.

1602

First mention of the inability to speak the Lord's Prayer as a proof of witchcraft occurs during a witchcraft examination in London.

1603

The author of *Daemonologie*, James VI of Scotland, becomes James I of England. Copies of Reginald Scot's book are ordered burned.

1604

Witchcraft Act of 1604 (King James I) is enacted. It greatly enlarges the scope of what is considered to be a witchcraft felony.

1605

Witchcraft trial occurs in Abingdon.

1612

Witchcraft trials occur in Lancashire.

1613

Witcraft trials occur in Sutton. First known case of a flotation test in England.

1619

Witchcraft trials occur in Lincoln.

1621

Witchcraft trials in London.
Witchcraft trials occur in Inverkiething.

1622

Witchcraft trials occur in Glasgow.

1624

Witchcraft trials occur in Bedford.

1627

A Guide to Grand Jury Men with Respect to Witches by Richard Bernard is published.

1630

Witchcraft trials occur in Lancaster and Kent.

1644

Matthew Hopkins, the self-proclaimed "Witch-Finder-General," becomes active.
Witchcraft trials occur in Norfolk and Chelmsford.

1647

Discovery of Witches by Matthew Hopkins is published. It was a very short treatise on how to identify witches, defending his methods of examination.

1649

Witchcraft trials occur at Newcastle and St. Albans.

1652

Witchcraft trials occur at Durham, Maidstone and Worcester.

1658

Witchcraft trials occur in Edinburgh.

1662

Witchcraft trails occur in Lowestoft.

1664

Witchcraft trials occur at Bury St. Edmonds.

1669

The Question of Witchcraft Debated by John Wagstaffe is published. Wagstaffe questioned truth of the alleged instances of witchcraft, stating that such accusations were "ridiculously absurd."

1678

Witchcraft trials occur at Prestonpans.

1682

Witchcraft trials occur in Exeter.

1697

Last mass execution of witches in Western Europe occurs in Paisley, Scotland.

1712

The last official conviction for witchcraft in England under the Witchcraft Act of 1604 occurs in Hertfordshire. Although convicted, the accused witch, Jane Wenham, was subsequently pardoned. An interesting detail of this last conviction is that the justice charged with her examination, Sir John Powell, instructed the jury to ignore any evidence of the accused witch flying because there was no law against flying.

1717

The last witchcraft trial in England ends in dismissal.

1727

The last execution for witchcraft in Scotland occurs.

1736

Witchcraft Act of 1604 is repealed and replaced by the Act of 1736. It remains in force until 1951.

Appendix D

VIRGINIA COUNTIES INVOLVED WITH WITCHCRAFT ACCUSATIONS, EXAMINATIONS AND RELATED SLANDER SUITS, 1626–1730

These are the known cases extracted from surviving records. As General Court cases would generally originate in a county court, both courts may be included in a single examination. Many of the instances of alleged witchcraft are backgrounds to slander suits.

The governor and/or governor's council at Jamestown and later Williamsburg heard the following cases:

ADMIRALTY COURT AT JAMESTOWN
1654: Investigation into death of Katherine Grady

GENERAL COURT AT JAMESTOWN
1626: Joan Wright
1641: Mrs. George Barker
1657: Barbara Wingbrough
1665: Alice Stephens
1668: Unknown woman and her child

GENERAL COURT AT WILLIAMSBURG
1706: Grace Sherwood (It is unclear whether the case was heard.)

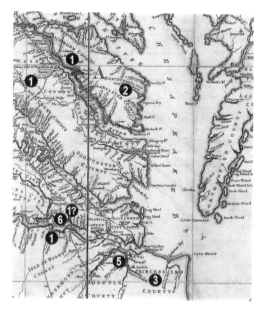

Recorded witchcraft cases and inquiries in Virginia, 1626–1730. *Author's collection.*

Justices of the peace of the various counties heard the following cases:

ESSEX COUNTY/KING AND QUEEN COUNTY
1695: Eleanor Morris and Nell Cane

LOWER NORFOLK COUNTY
1659: Mistress Robinson
1675: Joan Jenkins
1678/9: Alice Cartwrite

NORTHUMBERLAND COUNTY
1656: William Harding
1671: Hannah Neal

PRINCESS ANNE COUNTY
1697/8: Grace Sherwood
1698: John and Anne Byrd
1698: Grace Sherwood
1705/6, 1706: Grace Sherwood
1706: Alice Cornick

Richmond County
1730: Mary (indentured servant of John Samford)

Surry County
1626: Joan Wright

Westmoreland County
1694: Phyllis Money
1695: Elizabeth Dunkin

BIBLIOGRAPHY

Barstow, Anne Llewellyn. *Witchcraze: A New History of the European Witch Hunts*. San Francisco: HarperCollins, 1995.

Booth, Shirley Smith. *The Witches of Early America*. New York: Hastings House, 1975.

Bryson, William Hamilton. *Census of Law Books in Colonial Virginia*. Charlottesville: University Press of Virginia, 1978.

Burns, William E. *Witch Hunts in Europe and America: An Encyclopedia*. Westport, CT: Greenwood Press, 2003.

Burr, George L., ed. *Narratives of the Witchcraft Cases, 1648–1706*. New York: Barnes and Noble, 1975.

Cavendish, Richard. *The Black Arts*. New York: TarcherPerigee, 2017.

Coleman, Elizabeth Dabney. "The Witchcraft Delusion Rejected." *Virginia Cavalcade* 6, no. 1 (Summer 1956).

Dalton, Michael. *The Country Justice*. London, 1622.

Davies, Owen. "The Nightmare Experience, Sleep Paralysis, and Witchcraft Accusations." *Folklore* 114, no. 2 (August 2003): 181–203.

———. *Witchcraft, Magic and Culture, 1736–1951*. Manchester, UK: Manchester University Press, 1999.

Davis, Richard Beale. "The Devil in Virginia in the Seventeenth Century." *Virginia Magazine of History and Biography* 65, no. 2 (April 1957).

Dixon-Smith, Denise. "Concealed Shoes." *Archeological Leather Group Newsletter* 6 (1990).

Durston, Gregory. *Witchcraft and Witch Trials: A History of English Witchcraft and Its Legal Perspectives, 1542 to 1736.* Chichester, UK: Barry Rose Law Publishers, 2000.

Fair, Susan. *American Witches: A Broomstick Tour through Four Centuries.* New York: Skyhorse Publishing, 2016.

Gibson, Marion. *Reading Witchcraft: Stories of Early English Witches.* New York: Routledge, 1999.

————. *Witchcraft Myths in American Culture.* New York: Routledge, 2007.

Glanville, Joseph. *Saducismus Triumphatus.* London: S. Lownds, 1688.

Green, Marian. *Charms, Amulets, Talismans, & Spells.* New York: Bloomsbury Publishing, 2018.

Guiley, Rosemary. *The Encyclopedia of Witches and Witchcraft.* 2nd ed. New York: Checkmark Books, 1999.

Harsnett, Samuel. *A Declaration of Egregious Popish Impostures.* London: James Roberts, 1603.

Hoffer, Peter Charles, and William B. Scott, eds. *Criminal Proceedings in Colonial Virginia: Richmond County 1710/11 to 1754.* Athens: University of Georgia Press, 1984.

Hopkins, Matthew. *The Discovery of Witchcraft.* London: R. Royston, 1647.

Hutton, Ronald, ed. *Physical Evidence for Ritual Acts, Sorcery and Witchcraft in Christian Britain.* London: Palgrave MacMillan UK, 2015.

Jacob, Giles. *A New Law Dictionary.* 5th edition. London: Henry Lintot, 1744.

James VI and I. *Daemonologie.* Edinburgh: 1597; London: 1616.

Karlsen, Carol F. *The Devil in the Shape of a Woman: Witchcraft in Colonial New England.* New York: W.W. Norton & Company, 1987.

Kasti, Joe. *Malicious History: An Investigation into King James VI of Scotland & I of England and His Place in the History of Witch Hunts.* Newark, DE: Speedy Publishing, 2013.

Klaits, Joseph. *Servants of Satan: The Age of the Witch Hunts.* Bloomington: Indiana University Press, 1985.

Kyle, Louisa Venable. *The Witch of Pungo and Other Historical Stories of the Early Colonies.* Portsmouth, VA: Printcraft Press, 1973.

Linebaugh, Peter, and Marcus Rediker. *The Many-Headed Hydra: Sailors, Slaves, Commoners, and the Hidden History of the Revolutionary Atlantic.* Boston: Beacon Press, 2000.

MacGregor, Neil. *Shakespeare's Restless World: A Portrait of an Era in Twenty Objects.* New York: Penguin, 2012.

Mackay, Charles. *Extraordinary Popular Delusions and the Madness of Crowds.* New York: Harmony Books, 1980.

Martin, Lois. *The History of Witchcraft*. Edison, NJ: Chartwell Books, 2009.

Mather, Cotton. *The Wonders of the Invisible World*. New York: Dorset Press, 1991. Originally published 1692.

McCartney, Martha W. *Virginia Immigrants and Adventurers 1607–1635: A Biographical Dictionary*. Baltimore: Genealogical Publishing, 2007.

McIlwaine, H.R., ed. *Minutes of the Council and General Court of Colonial Virginia 1622–1632, 1670–1676*. 2nd edition. Richmond: Virginia State Library, 1979.

Meltzer, Milton. *Witches and Witch-hunts: A History of Persecution*. New York: Blue Sky Press, 1999.

Morton, Richard L. *Colonial Virginia*. Vol. 2, *Westward Expansion and Prelude to Revolution*. Chapel Hill: University of North Carolina Press, 1960.

Oldridge, Darren. *The Devil in Tudor and Stuart England*. Stroud, UK: History Press, 2010.

Perkins, William. *A Discourse on the Damned Art of Witchcraft*. London, 1608.

Price, William S., Jr., ed. *North Carolina Higher-Court Records 1702–1708*. 2nd series, vol. 4. Raleigh: North Carolina State University Print Shop, 1974.

Rankin, Hugh F. *Criminal Trial Proceedings in the General Court of Colonial Virginia*. Williamsburg, VA: Colonial Williamsburg Foundation, 1965.

Salgado, Gamini. *The Elizabethan Underworld*. Gloucestershire, UK: Alan Sutton Publishing Ltd., 1992.

Salmon, Emily J., and Edward D.C. Campbell Jr. *Hornbook of Virginia History*. 4th edition. Richmond: Library of Virginia, 1994.

Scot, Reginald. *The Discoverie of Witchcraft*. New York: Dover Publications, 1972. Originally published 1584.

Sharpe, James. *Instruments of Darkness: Witchcraft in England 1550–1750*. London: Hamish Hamilton Ltd., 1996.

———. *Witchcraft in Early Modern England*. London: Pearson Education, 2001.

Thurston. Robert W. *Witch, Wicce, Mother Goose: The Rise and Fall of Witch Hunts in Europe and North America*. London: Longman, 2001.

Turner, Florence Kimberly. *Gateway to the World: A History of Princess Anne County, Virginia, 1607–1824*. Easley, SC: Southern Historical Press, 1984.

Webb, George. *The Office and Authority of a Justice of Peace*. Williamsburg, VA: William Parks, 1736.

Webster, John. *The Displaying of Supposed Witchcraft*. London: JM, 1677.

Wedeck, Harry, E. *A Treasury of Witchcraft*. New York: Gramercy Books, 1961.

Whitaker, Alexander. *Good Newes from Virginia*. 1613. New York: Scholars' Facsimiles & Reprints, 1936.

Williams, Selma R. *Riding the Nightmare: Women & Witchcraft from the Old World to Colonial Salem*. New York: Harper Perennial, 1978.

Wilson, Derek K. *A Magical World: Superstition and Science from the Renaissance to the Enlightenment*. New York: Pegasus Books, 2018.

Witkowski, Monica C. "Grace Sherwood (ca. 1660–1740)." *Encyclopedia Virginia*. Virginia Foundation for the Humanities, January 1, 2014. Web. November 27, 2018.

INDEX

ABOUT THE AUTHOR

Carson Hudson has been passionate about history since he was a young boy growing up in Virginia, surrounded by Civil War battlefields. He is a practicing military and social historian, author, Emmy Award–winning screenwriter and circus fire-eater. He lectures regularly at museums and colleges on a wide variety of subjects, but his particular interests are the Civil War and colonial witchcraft. He performs regularly as part of the old-time music duo Hudson & Clark and with the Cigar Box String Band. In his spare time, he likes to sleep.

Visit us at
www.historypress.com